# Ancestors of Franklin Eugene Timms

### Generation 1

1. **Franklin Eugene Timms**, son of John Martin Timms and Lillie Louise Pierce was born on 03 May 1940 in Dundas, Ohio. He married **Evlyn Marie Stewart**. She was born on 17 Dec 1944 in South Perry, Ohio.

### Generation 2

2. **John Martin Timms**, son of Charles Vance Timms and Maggie Elizabeth Martin was born on 27 Feb 1919 in Vinton County, Ohio. He died on 10 Aug 1946 in Vinton County, Ohio. He married **Lillie Louise Pierce**.

3. **Lillie Louise Pierce**, daughter of Franklin Pierce and Lola Castor was born on 07 Jul 1923 in Ohio. She died on 23 May 2006 in Vinton County, Ohio.

Notes for John Martin Timms:
Killed in an accidental explosion at Austin Powder Company in Vinton County, Ohio.

Lillie Louise Pierce and John Martin Timms had the following child:

1.      i. Franklin Eugene Timms, son of John Martin Timms and Lillie Louise Pierce was born on 03 May 1940 in Dundas, Ohio. He married Evlyn Marie Stewart. She was born on 17 Dec 1944 in South Perry, Ohio.

### Generation 3

4. **Charles Vance Timms**, son of Ezra Quimby Timms and Susan Minerva Barnett was born on 19 Dec 1875 in Vinton County, Ohio. He died on 01 Mar 1961 in Hocking County, Ohio. He married **Maggie Elizabeth Martin**, daughter of Albert Martin and Mary Alice (unknown) on 01 Jan 1918 in Vinton County, Ohio.

5. **Maggie Elizabeth Martin**, daughter of Albert Martin and Mary Alice (unknown) was born on 03 Jan 1889 in Vinton County, Ohio. She died on 17 Jan 1939 in Clinton, Vinton County, Ohio.

More About Charles Vance Timms:
Burial: Hixon Cemetery, Vinton County, Ohio
Occupation: Farmer, Vinton County, Ohio

More About Maggie Elizabeth Martin:
Burial: 19 Jan 1939 in Hixon Cemetery, Vinton County,
Ohio Cause Of Death: Bowel Obstruction

Maggie Elizabeth Martin and Charles Vance Timms had the following children:

2.      i. John Martin Timms, son of Charles Vance Timms and Maggie Elizabeth Martin was born on 27 Feb 1919 in Vinton County, Ohio. He died on 10 Aug 1946 in Vinton County, Ohio. He married Lillie Louise Pierce. She was born on 07 Jul 1923 in Ohio. She died on 23 May 2006 in Vinton County, Ohio.

     ii. Alice Minerva Timms, daughter of Charles Vance Timms and Maggie Elizabeth Martin was born on 18 Apr 1921 in Vinton County, Ohio. She died on 25 Oct 1953 in Dundas, Ohio.

More About Alice Minerva Timms:
Burial: 27 Oct 1953 in Hixon Cemetery, Dundas, Ohio

6. **Franklin Pierce**, son of Pinkney Pierce and Malinda Gold was born on 30 Nov 1890 in

I0775937

Vinton, Vinton County, Ohio. He died on 16 Jun 1953 in Clinton, Vinton County, Ohio. He married **Lola Castor**, daughter of Elias Charles Castor and Loveta Eakin on 29 Mar 1913 in Vinton, Vinton County, Ohio.

7.      **Lola Castor**, daughter of Elias Charles Castor and Loveta Eakin was born on 03 Dec 1895 in Vales Mills, Vinton County, Ohio. She died on 17 Dec 1958 in Vinton County, Ohio.

More About Franklin Pierce:
Burial: 18 Jun 1953 in Radcliff Cemetery, Vinton County,
Ohio Cause Of Death: Lymph Sarcoma
Occupation: Farmer
Occupation: Brick Maker

Notes for Franklin Pierce:
World War One Draft registration gives November 30, 1891 as birth date. Death certificate has November 30, 1890 as birth date. 1900 U.S. census has November 1890 as birth date.

Lola Castor and Franklin Pierce had the following children:

i.    Malinda Lovina Pierce, daughter of Franklin Pierce and Lola Castor was born on 02 Nov 1913 in McArthur, Ohio. She died on 12 Jul 1935 in Athens, Ohio. She married (unknown) Eberts. She married (unknown) Nettles.

More About Malinda Lovina Pierce:
Burial: 14 Jul 1935 in Radcliff Cemetery, Vinton County,
Ohio Cause Of Death: Ruptured Appendix and peritonitis.

ii.    Alvin Pierce, son of Franklin Pierce and Lola Castor was born about 1915.

iii.    Evelyn Pierce, daughter of Franklin Pierce and Lola Castor was born about 1917.

iv.    Howard Pierce, son of Franklin Pierce and Lola Castor was born about 1920.

v.    Leo Pierce, son of Franklin Pierce and Lola Castor was born about 1924.

4.    vi. Lillie Louise Pierce, daughter of Franklin Pierce and Lola Castor was born on 07 Jul 1923 in Ohio. She died on 23 May 2006 in Vinton County, Ohio. She married John Martin Timms. He was born on 27 Feb 1919 in Vinton County, Ohio. He died on 10 Aug 1946 in Vinton County, Ohio. She married James McManis.

vii. Edith Pierce, daughter of Franklin Pierce and Lola Castor was born about 1926.

viii. Delbert Clayton Pierce, son of Franklin Pierce and Lola Castor was born on 10 Jun 1933 in Vinton County, Ohio. He died on 30 Jan 1934 in Clinton, Vinton County, Ohio.

More About Delbert Clayton Pierce:
Burial: 31 Jan 1934 in Radcliff Cemetery, Vinton County, Ohio
Cause Of Death: Pneumonia

---

## Generation 4

8.      **Ezra Quimby Timms**, son of Richard Timms and Elizabeth Bibbee was born on 19 Sep 1842 in Wirt County, Virginia. He died on 15 Aug 1925 in Clinton Township, Vinton County, Ohio. He

married **Susan Minerva Barnett** , daughter of George William Barnett and Sarah Rockhold on 26 Oct 1865 in Wood County, West Virginia.

9.    **Susan Minerva Barnett**, daughter of George William Barnett and Sarah Rockhold was born on 28 Nov 1845 in Wood County, Virginia. She died on 15 Feb 1922 in Columbus, Ohio.


More About Ezra Quimby Timms:
Burial: 16 Aug 1925 in Hixon Cemetery, Vinton County,
Ohio Living In: 1880 Clinton, Vinton County, Ohio
Occupation: Farmer
Military Service: Bet. 15 Aug 1862-17 Jun 1865; Company F, 11th West Virginia Infantry, U.S.A. (Civil War)
Military Service: 07 Sep 1864; Promoted to Sergeant in Company F, 11th West Virginia Infantry.


Notes for Ezra Quimby Timms:
SOURCE: Vinton County Newspaper McArthur Democrat Enquirer August 19, 1925 "Death of Ezra Q. Timms"

"Ezra Quimby Timms aged 82 years died at his home in Dundas, Ohio Sunday August 15, at 4 o'clock. He was a Civil War veteran, sergeant in Co K. 11th West Virginia Infantry, serving about three years until the end of the war. A couple of sketches as to his arduous and patriotic services during these trying times were published in this paper during the past year. He was a man of fine capacity, a successful farmer and raiser of fine livestock in which he took commendable pride and was universally respected for his sterling qualities as a man and citizen.
Surviving are the following named children, grandchildren, and great grand children; his daughter Mrs. Amy Salts of Dundas, her daughter Lulu Smith of Marion: daughter Ina Workman of Dundas; daughter Sybil Timms at Home: Sons of Amy Salts: Roy, Kenneth and Earl Salts of Detroit; Otto of Portsmouth Robert and Garvin at Dundas; son Henry Timms his daughter Helen; his son James W. Timms, Dundas, his daughter Mrs Alta Perriner of Cleveland, her daughter Betty Jane daughter Annie Russell, wife of Sam Russell of Dundas, their daughter Nellie Dye wife of Roy Dye; son of Charles Timms, his son John and daughter Alice, Dundas, two children of his son George (deceased) Barnet Timms of Wellsburg, West Virginia and daughter Blanche Timms of Milwaukee, Wis., daughter Mrs Jennie Bay wife of Earl Bay, their children Virginia, Charlene, Robert and Julian Richard;
The great grandchildren of deceased are Ralph and Mary Smith children of Lulu Smith; Louise and Marie Workman, children of Ina Workman; Russell and Theresa Dye, children of Nellie Dye; Betty Jane Perriner before mentioned. Ida daughter of Ezra Timms who was the wife of M.S. Cox has been deceased for a number of years.
The funeral was at 2 o'clock on Monday afternoon at the residence, Rev. O.J. Howearth of Nelsonville and Dr. Taylor of McArthur officiating. Burial in the Hixon cemetery near Dundas, P. Gaskill undertaker. The Pall bearers were members of the American Legion: Dr H.S. James, Herbert Hamilton, Eura Frazee, Fred Button, James Warren, F.E. Weinrich. The honorary pall bearers were Civil War Veterans: Dr. C.B. Taylor, Capt. D.H. Moore, V.R. Sprague, Richard Clements, John Glover, John Franklin and Robert Hayes."

OBITUARY

Ezra Quimby Timms born September 19,1842 died August 15, 1925 aged 82 years 10 months and 27 days.
Mr. Timms was the son of Richard and Elizabeth Timms was born in Wirt County Virginia, which is now West Virginia, spending his boyhood days

among his native hills. Securing a district school education and training
himself as a farmer. When 20 years old he enlisted in the 11th W. Va.
Infantry in the Union Army. This regiment was assigned to special duty
and helped to win the hard battles of Cedar Creek and Winchester.

Mr. Timms witnessed the dashing ride of that gallant Phil Sheridan in the
Cedar Creek fight. At Petersburg the regiment was almost killed and wounded.
Mr. Timms serving almost 3 years continuous duty and fighting was never
wounded nor in a hospital. At Spencer in Roane County, Viginia he was captured
and paroled the next day and honorably discharged June 17, 1865. In the fall of
1865 his father sold the home place in Virginia and moved to Dundas and bought
452 acres of land where Dundas now stands. Mr. Timms father died October
1875, his mother in March 1876. In the meantime he had returned to his native
county and state and married Susan M. Barnett on October 26, 1865 who died
the 15th of February 1922. To them were born 8 children, 20 grandchildren, and
7 great grandchildren. The children were:
Amy L., who married Willis G. Salts
Anna L., who married Samuel
Russel
Geneva E., who married Earl Bay
Ida B, who married M. S. Cox
and the four sons Henry M., James W.,  Charles V. and George B.

Mr Timms united with the Christian Church at Bethel August 10, 1894 and
retained his membership until his death. To this community the people have lost a true and
sincere friend and neighbor; a patriotic citizen. Faithful to his duty, his friends numbered by his
large acquaintance all of whom testify to his noble character and
splendid citizenship. We cherish the memory of E.Q. Timms because of
his stainless record and the life he has lived among us.
We cannot at this time bid farewell to Sergeant Timms without paying a
tribute to his army record as he is the last one of the Civil War veterans in our
neighborhood. "Soldier rest! thy warfare is o'er
Sleep the sleep that knows no breaking
Dream of battlefields no more,'
Days of danger, nights of waking,
In our isle's enchanted hall
Hands unseen they couch are
strewing, Fairy strains of music fall,
Every sense in slumber dewing.
Sergeant Timms, rest! thy warfare is
o'er, Dream of fighting fields no more;
Morn of toil, nor night of waking."

"CARD OF THANKS"
"We, the children of E.Q. Timms feel grateful to the friends, neighbors,
those who furnished flowers and music at the funeral of our father, and
take this means of thanking all.
The Children"
**************************************************************************
SOURCE: Vinton County Newspaper McArthur Democrat Enquirer June 10, 1925

"Sergeant Ezra Q. Timms of Dundas, 11th West Virginia Infantry, Civil War
was a pleasant caller in our office Monday. Mr. Timms still has a
remarkable accurate memory of events which he came in contact during
"The Great Unpleasantness".
He thinks that he and John Franklin of McArthur, late of Co. F. 36th Ohio Inf.
are the only Vinton County soldiers now living who were present at the
surrender of LEe and his army at Appomattox, Virginia in April 1865. He says
the Confederate soldiers appeared to be rejoiced that the war was over. At the
surrender, they got a good feed from the Union soldiers. The "rebs" were

so hungry and exhausted that they could not walk 50 yards without sitting down. There were men of all ages among them from 15 to 60 years old. They were without either money or provisions, and how they ever got to their distant homes has always remained a myster to Sergeant Timms. He and Mr. Franklin were both present at the famous battle of Cedar Creek, October 19, 1864 when Sheridan rode furiously up to the fiedl from "Twenty Miles Away". A prisoner taken later, told how General Jubal Early, the confederate commander took the defeat. After the battle he tried to halt the retreat of his forces at Fisher's Hill, a long ridge connecting Massanutten Mountain with North Mountain. He sat on his horse beseeching his troppst o half and form a line of defense. "Boys won't you rally once more for all Jubal?" "Nary a rally, Jubal" replied the discouraged troopers and so ended the fighting in the Shenandoah Valley."

-------------------------------------------------------------------------------------------------

Ezra Timms marriage record states he was born in Wood County, Virginia instead of Wirt County, Virginia.
-------------------------------------------------------------------------------------------------
Enlisted in Company F, 11th West Virginia Infantry, U.S. Army, at Newark, Virginia on August 15, 1862.
-------------------------------------------------------------------------------------------------
Mustered out of Company F, 11th West Virginia Infantry at Richmond, Virginia on June 17, 1865.
-------------------------------------------------------------------------------------------------




More About Susan Minerva Barnett:
Burial: 17 Feb 1922 in Hixon Cemetery, Vinton County, Ohio
Cause Of Death: Liver Cancer

Susan Minerva Barnett and Ezra Quimby Timms had the following children:
    i.    Amy Louise Timms, daughter of Ezra Quimby Timms and Susan Minerva Barnett was born on 24 Mar 1868 in Clinton Township, Vinton County, Ohio. She died on 04 May 1959 in Vinton County, Ohio. She married Willis Garvin Salts, son of John Salts and Ivy Hoffiner on 21 Jun 1888 in Vinton County, Ohio. He was born on 02 Mar 1863 in Vinton County, Ohio. He died on 10 Nov 1910 in Vinton County, Ohio.

    More About Amy Louise Timms:
    Burial: Hixon Cemetery, Vinton County, Ohio


    More About Willis Garvin Salts:
    Burial: 12 Nov 1910 in Hixon Cemetery, Vinton County, Ohio
    Occupation: Farmer


    ii.    Henry Milton Timms, son of Ezra Quimby Timms and Susan Minerva Barnett was born on 31 Mar 1870 in Dundas, Vinton County, Ohio. He died on 15 Feb 1953 in Wellston, Ohio. He married Anna Gunning, daughter of Orville Gunning and Catherine (unknown) on 29 Mar 1889. She was born on 23 Oct 1864 in Vinton County, Ohio. She died on 17 Jun 1943 in Clinton, Vinton County, Ohio.

    More About Henry Milton Timms:
    Burial: 18 Feb 1953 in Elk Cemetery, McArthur, Ohio

Cause Of Death:  Gangrene of left leg
Occupation: Farmer


More About Anna Gunning:
Burial: 20 Jun 1943 in Elk Cemetery, McArthur, Ohio



iii.     James W. Timms, son of Ezra Quimby Timms and Susan Minerva Barnett was born on 09 Mar 1872 in Clinton Township, Vinton County, Ohio. He died on 02 Mar 1961. He married Sarah J. Bobo, daughter of Thomas W. Bobo and Mary E. (unknown) on 30 Jan 1895 in Vinton County, Ohio. She was born about 1865 in Ohio.


More    About    James    W.
Timms:
Occupation:  Farmer

iv.     Anna Luella Timms, daughter of Ezra Quimby Timms and Susan Minerva Barnett was born on 23 Dec 1873 in Clinton Township, Vinton County, Ohio. She died on 02 Jan 1949 in Clinton Township, Vinton County, Ohio. She married Samuel Russell on 01 Jan 1896 in Vinton County, Ohio. He died after 02 Jan 1949.


More About Anna Luella Timms:
Burial: 05 Jan 1949 in Elk Cemetery, McArthur, Ohio
Cause Of Death:  Cerebral Hemorrhage

4.      v. Charles Vance Timms, son of Ezra Quimby Timms and Susan Minerva Barnett was born on 19 Dec 1875 in Vinton County, Ohio. He died on 01 Mar 1961 in Hocking County, Ohio. He married Maggie Elizabeth Martin, daughter of Albert Martin and Mary Alice (unknown) on 01 Jan 1918 in Vinton County, Ohio. She was born on 03 Jan 1889 in Vinton County, Ohio. She died on 17 Jan 1939 in Clinton, Vinton County, Ohio.

vi.     George Barnett Timms, son of Ezra Quimby Timms and Susan Minerva Barnett was born on 29 Jul 1878 in Dundas, Clinton Township, Vinton County, Ohio. He died on 10 Sep 1916. He married Irma Pierce on 06 Sep 1902. He married Sadie Wortman on 17 Sep 1907 in Hamilton, Ohio. He married Sarah Elizabeth Monroe, daughter of Charles B. Monroe and Eliza Westcott on 17 Sep 1907 in Cincinnati, Ohio. She was born on 13 Feb 1878 in Tuscola, Illinois. She died on 07 Jul 1940.


More About George Barnett Timms:
Occupation:  Railroad, Freeport, Illinois


Notes for Sadie Wortman:
Ohio Marriage Records gives name as Sadie Enlow.


vii.    Ida Blanche Timms, daughter of Ezra Quimby Timms and Susan Minerva Barnett was born on 02 Aug 1883 in Dundas, Vinton County, Ohio. She died on 17 Jun 1915 in Los Angeles, California. She married Milton Shed Cox, son of James G. Cox and Nancy Graves on 24 Apr 1913 in Cincinnati, Ohio. He was born in 1868 in Vinton County, Ohio.

More About Milton Shed Cox:
Occupation: Yardmaster, Santa Fe Railroad, Los Angeles, California

    viii.    Susan Geneva Timms, daughter of Ezra Quimby Timms and Susan Minerva Barnett was born on 04 Feb 1886 in Dundas, Vinton County, Ohio. She died on 24 Apr 1948 in McArthur, Ohio. She married Earl C. Bay, son of F. H. Bay and Ida Trimmer on 20 Dec 1906 in Vinton County, Ohio. He was born in 1880 in Hamden. He died before 24 Apr 1948.

More About Susan Geneva Timms:
Burial: 27 Apr 1948 in McArthur, Ohio
Cause Of Death: Cerebral Hemorrhage

More About Earl C. Bay:
Occupation: Farmer

10.    **Albert Martin**, son of Harrison Martin and (unknown) was born on 06 Jun 1867 in Virginia. He died on 15 Mar 1935 in Clinton, Vinton County, Ohio. He married **Mary Alice (unknown)**.

11.    **Mary Alice (unknown)**.

More About Albert Martin:
Burial: 17 Mar 1935 in Ridgewood Cemetery, Wellston,
Ohio Cause Of Death: Pneumonia

Mary Alice (unknown) and Albert Martin had the following child:

5.    i.    Maggie Elizabeth Martin, daughter of Albert Martin and Mary Alice (unknown) was born on 03 Jan 1889 in Vinton County, Ohio. She died on 17 Jan 1939 in Clinton, Vinton County, Ohio. She married Charles Vance Timms, son of Ezra Quimby Timms and Susan Minerva Barnett on 01 Jan 1918 in Vinton County, Ohio. He was born on 19 Dec 1875 in Vinton County, Ohio. He died on 01 Mar 1961 in Hocking County, Ohio.

12.    **Pinkney Pierce**, son of William J. Pierce and Hannah Gregory was born on 03 Oct 1855 in Radcliff, Vinton County, Ohio. He died on 17 Dec 1936 in Gallipolis, Ohio. He married **Malinda Gold** on 06 Feb 1879 in Vinton County, Ohio.

13.    **Malinda Gold** was born on 05 Dec 1857 in Radcliff, Vinton County, Ohio. She died on 17 Oct 1943 in Vinton County, Ohio.

More About Pinkney Pierce:
Burial: 20 Dec 1936 in Ratcliff, Vinton County,
Ohio
Cause Of Death: Gangrene of Right Leg
Occupation: Farmer

More About Malinda Gold:
Burial: 19 Oct 1943 in Radcliff Cemetery, Vinton County,
Ohio
Cause Of Death: Fractured Neck

Malinda Gold and Pinkney Pierce had the following children:

i.    Minnie G. Pierce, daughter of Pinkney Pierce and Malinda Gold was born on 05 Nov 1879 in Hocking County, Ohio.

ii.    Della Mae Pierce, daughter of Pinkney Pierce and Malinda Gold was born on 04 Jul 1882 in McArthur, Vinton County, Ohio. She died on 11 Apr 1946 in Wilkesville, Ohio. She married William Long.

More About Della Mae Pierce:
Burial: 13 Apr 1946 in Radcliff Cemetery, Vinton County, Ohio Cause Of Death: ; Gastric Carcinoma

iii.    Emma Pierce, daughter of Pinkney Pierce and Malinda Gold was born on 25 Jul 1883 in Vinton, Vinton County, Ohio.

iv.    Elizabeth Belle Pierce, daughter of Pinkney Pierce and Malinda Gold was born on 15 Apr 1886 in Vinton, Vinton County, Ohio. She married Charles Ginn, son of John Ginn and Rachel Ireland on 13 Aug 1903 in Vinton, Vinton County, Ohio. He was born in 1883 in Radcliff, Vinton County, Ohio.

v.    Hannah Elizabeth Pierce, daughter of Pinkney Pierce and Malinda Gold was born on 28 Feb 1888 in Vinton, Vinton County, Ohio. She married Forest Zinn, son of George Zinn and Roberta McDaniel on 25 Jul 1908 in Vinton County, Ohio. He was born on 07 Jun 1886 in Radcliff, Vinton County, Ohio.

vi.    William Pierce, son of Pinkney Pierce and Malinda Gold was born on 01 May 1889 in Vinton, Vinton County, Ohio.

6.    vii. Franklin Pierce, son of Pinkney Pierce and Malinda Gold was born on 30 Nov 1890 in Vinton, Vinton County, Ohio. He died on 16 Jun 1953 in Clinton, Vinton County, Ohio. He married Lola Castor, daughter of Elias Charles Castor and Loveta Eakin on 29 Mar 1913 in Vinton, Vinton County, Ohio. She was born on 03 Dec 1895 in Vales Mills, Vinton County, Ohio. She died on 17 Dec 1958 in Vinton County, Ohio.

viii.    Lucinda Pierce, daughter of Pinkney Pierce and Malinda Gold was born on 17 Aug 1892 in Vinton, Vinton County, Ohio. She married Herbert Norton, son of Seth J. Norton and Anna Marstin on 26 Mar 1910 in Vinton, Vinton County, Ohio. He was born in 1888 in Radcliff, Vinton County, Ohio.

ix.    Ida Pierce, daughter of Pinkney Pierce and Malinda Gold was born on 07 Sep 1894 in Vinton, Vinton County, Ohio. She married James Chester Yates, son of Benjamin Yates and Alice Henry on 13 Aug 1913 in Vinton County, Ohio. He was born in 1894.

14.    **Elias Charles Castor**, son of Louis Castor and Melvina Martin was born on 25 Jan 1871 in Meigs County, Ohio. He died on 30 Sep 1952 in Elk Township, Vinton County, Ohio. He married **Loveta Eakin**, daughter of Joseph Eakin and Hulda Lane on 26 May 1894 in Vinton County, Ohio.

15.    **Loveta Eakin**, daughter of Joseph Eakin and Hulda Lane was born in Jul 1876 in July Ohio. She died on 14 Mar 1916 in Elk Township, Vinton County, Ohio.
More About Elias Charles Castor:
Burial: 03 Oct 1952 in Caster Cemetery, Meigs County, Ohio
Cause Of Death: Coronary Occlusion
Living In: 1910 Columbia Township, Meigs county, Ohio
Occupation: 1910 Rail Road Tie Maker

Occupation:  Coal Miner

More About Loveta Eakin:
Burial: 17 Mar 1916 in Caster Cemetery, Meigs County, Ohio
Cause Of Death:  Complications during child birth.

Loveta Eakin and Elias Charles Castor had the following children:

7.    i.  Lola Castor, daughter of Elias Charles Castor and Loveta Eakin was born on 03 Dec 1895 in Vales Mills, Vinton County, Ohio. She died on 17 Dec 1958 in Vinton County, Ohio. She married Franklin Pierce, son of Pinkney Pierce and Malinda Gold on 29 Mar 1913 in Vinton, Vinton County, Ohio. He was born on 30 Nov 1890 in Vinton, Vinton County, Ohio. He died on 16 Jun 1953 in Clinton, Vinton County, Ohio.

      ii.  Bryan Marion Castor, son of Elias Charles Castor and Loveta Eakin was born on 03 Mar 1897 in Vales Mill, Vinton County, Ohio. He died on 05 Sep 1977 in Athens, Ohio. He married Edna Hoyd about 1917. She was born on 03 Jul 1898 in Knox Township, vinton County, Ohio. She died on 05 Sep 1980 in Chillicothe, Ohio.

           More About Bryan Marion Castor:
           Living In: 1930  Elk Township, Vinton County, Ohio
           Military Service: Bet. 26 Aug 1918-15 Jul 1919; U.S Army, World War One

      iii.  Leone Mabel Castor, daughter of Elias Charles Castor and Loveta Eakin was born in Jun 1899 in Ohio. She died in 1998.

      iv.  Earl Castor, son of Elias Charles Castor and Loveta Eakin was born about 1901 in Ohio. He died in 1968.

      v.  Merle R. Castor, son of Elias Charles Castor and Loveta Eakin was born in 1902 in Ohio. He died in 1972.

      vi.  Arnett Castor, son of Elias Charles Castor and Loveta Eakin was born in 1904 in Ohio. He died in 1967.

      vii.  Lewis Henry Castor, son of Elias Charles Castor and Loveta Eakin was born about 1907 in Ohio. He died in 1970.

      viii.  Dorena L. Castor, daughter of Elias Charles Castor and Loveta Eakin was born about Apr 1909 in Ohio. She died in 1994.

---

### Generation 5

16.    **Richard Timms**, son of John B. Timms and Nancy Davis was born on 13 Jan 1804 in Loudoun County, Virginia. He died on 16 Oct 1878 in Dundas, Vinton County, Ohio. He married **Elizabeth Bibbee**, daughter of John E. Bibbee and Elizabeth Spaecht on 01 Nov 1832 in Wood County, Virginia.

17.    **Elizabeth Bibbee**, daughter of John E. Bibbee and Elizabeth Spaecht was born on 21 Nov 1805 in Wood County, Virginia. She died on 25 Mar 1879 in Dundas, Ohio.

      More About Richard Timms:
      Burial: Elk Cemetery, McArthur,
      Ohio
      Occupation: Innkeeper
      Occupation: Farmer

---

More About Elizabeth Bibbee:
Burial: Elk Cemetery, McArthur, Ohio


Notes for Elizabeth Bibbee:
"TIMMS- Elizabeth Timms, wife of the late Richard Timms, was born in Wood County, West Virginia November 21, 1805 and died at McArthur Station ,Vinton County Ohio on March 25th, 1879. In the 74th years of her age. She united with the M.E. Church when young and lived a faithful and true Christian to the end. For five years she had been an invalid. During three years her afflictions were many and great; but through all, she bore up with marked patience, never once having been heard to complain. In their many afflictions, this much afflicted family have the sympathies of many friends.
      And may the members of this family who yet remain, emulate the spirit of their sainted mother and like her through the grace of our Lord Jesus Christ, receive a crown of eternal life. JCA."



Elizabeth Bibbee and Richard Timms had the following children:

i.   Harriet L. Timms, daughter of Richard Timms and Elizabeth Bibbee was born on 17 Sep 1833 in Virginia. She died on 18 Nov 1865 in West Virginia. She married James William Morehead, son of Nathaniel H. Morehead and Mary Richards on 12 Dec 1856 in Virginia. He was born in May 1826 in Wood County, Virginia. He died in 1909.

ii.  Mary Jane Timms, daughter of Richard Timms and Elizabeth Bibbee was born on 18 Jan 1836 in Virginia. She died on 16 Jun 1917 in Vinton County, Ohio. She married Charles Wesley Barnett, son of George William Barnett and Sarah Rockhold on 21 May 1861 in Wood County, Virginia. He was born on 16 Feb 1834 in Wood County, Virginia. He died on 06 Jun 1903 in Oskaloosa, Iowa.

     More About Mary Jane Timms:
     Burial: Elk Cemetery, McArthur, Ohio


     More About Charles Wesley Barnett:
     Burial: Elk Cemetery, McArthur, Ohio



iii. John Bibbee Timms, son of Richard Timms and Elizabeth Bibbee was born on 18 Feb 1838 in Wirt County, Virginia. He died on 02 Oct 1911 in Clinton, Vinton County, Ohio. He married Roseanna Barnes, daughter of John Barnes and Frances Davis on 24 Sep 1863 in Wirt County, West Virginia. She was born on 30 Apr 1844 in Wirt County, Virginia. She died on 15 Apr 1927 in Vinton County, Ohio.

     More About John Bibbee Timms:
     Burial: Elk Cemetery, McArthur, Ohio
     Cause Of Death: Muscular Rheumatism
     Living In: 1880 Clinton, Vinton County, Ohio
     Occupation:  Farmer


     More About Roseanna Barnes:
     Burial: 17 Apr 1927 in Elk Cemetery, McArthur, Ohio

iv.     Charles W. Timms, son of Richard Timms and Elizabeth Bibbee was born on 19 Dec 1839 in Wirt County, Virginia. He died on 04 Nov 1906 in Dundas, Vinton County, Ohio. He married Charlotte Elizabeth Dowd, daughter of John Dowd and Olive Fuller on 11 Oct 1877 in McArthur, Vinton County, Ohio. She was born on 17 Jan 1857 in Vinton County, Ohio. She died on 12 Dec 1934 in Vinton County, Ohio.

More About Charles W. Timms:
Burial: 06 Nov 1906 in Elk Cemetery, McArthur, Ohio
Military Service: Bet. 15 Aug 1862-17 Jun 1865 ; Company F, 11th West Virginia Infantry, U.S.A. (Civil War)
Military Service: 11 Sep 1864; Promoted to Corporal in Company F, 11th West Virginia Infantry

Notes for Charles W. Timms:
SOURCE: Vinton County, Ohio Newspaper McArthur Democrat Enquirer November 8, 1906

"Charles W. Timms, an honorable citizen and brave soldier, died November 4, at his home in Dundas, aged 66 years, 10 months and 15 days. He was born in West Virginia and served three years as corporal of Company F of the 11th West Virginia Infantry, being at Cedar Creek and many other battles.

He has been a resident of Dundas for 41 years. He was married to Charlotte E. Dowd in 1877. He leaves a widow, two sons and a daughter, brother and sister and a host of relatives and friends, sincere mourners of his departure.

Funeral services took place at the home on November 6th conducted by Dr. Taylor. Old comrades carried him to his grave in Elk Cemetery. A very large concourse of people attended the services

---------------------------------------------------------------------------------------------------

Enlisted in Company F, 11th West Virginia Infantry, U.S. Army, at Newark, Virginia on August 15th, 1862.
Mustered out of Company F, 11th West Virginia Infantry at Richmond, Virginia on June 17, 1865.

More About Charlotte Elizabeth Dowd:
Burial: Elk Cemetery, McArthur, Ohio

8.     v. Ezra Quimby Timms, son of Richard Timms and Elizabeth Bibbee was born on 19 Sep 1842 in Wirt County, Virginia. He died on 15 Aug 1925 in Clinton Township, Vinton County, Ohio. He married Susan Minerva Barnett, daughter of George William Barnett and Sarah Rockhold on 26 Oct 1865 in Wood County, West Virginia. She was born on 28 Nov 1845 in Wood County, Virginia. She died on 15 Feb 1922 in Columbus, Ohio.

vi.     Sarah Margaret Timms, daughter of Richard Timms and Elizabeth Bibbee was born on 15 May 1844 in Wirt County, Virginia. She died on 23 Dec 1921 in Mahaska County, Iowa. She married Joseph Harvey Evans, son of Jacob Evans and Mary (unknown) on 25 Nov 1886 in Mahaska County, Iowa. He was born on 10 Aug 1822 in Maryland. He died on 09 Jul 1908 in Oskaloosa, Mahaska County, Iowa.

More About Sarah Margaret Timms:
Burial: Coal Creek Cemetery, Mahaska, Iowa


More About Joseph Harvey Evans:
Burial: Coal Creek Cemetery, Mahaska, Iowa



    vii.    Frances B. Timms, daughter of Richard Timms and Elizabeth Bibbee was born on 08 Jun 1848 in Virginia. She died in 1920 in Long Beach, California. She married William S. England on 24 Mar 1869 in Vinton County, Ohio.

18.    **George William Barnett** was born on 17 Jun 1803 in Wood County, Virginia. He died on 29 Aug 1885 in Wood County, West Virginia. He married **Sarah Rockhold**, daughter of Charles Rockhold and Permelia Wright on 02 Oct 1828 in Wood County, Virginia.

19.    **Sarah Rockhold**, daughter of Charles Rockhold and Permelia Wright was born on 26 Feb 1802 in Wirt County, Virginia. She died on 03 Oct 1890.


More About George William Barnett:
Burial: Barnett Cemetery, Wood County, West Virginia


More About Sarah Rockhold:
Burial: Barnett Cemetery, Wood County, West Virginia

Sarah Rockhold and George William Barnett had the following children:
    i.    Alphina Barnett, daughter of George William Barnett and Sarah Rockhold was born about 1832 in Virginia.

    ii.    Charles Wesley Barnett, son of George William Barnett and Sarah Rockhold was born on 16 Feb 1834 in Wood County, Virginia. He died on 06 Jun 1903 in Oskaloosa, Iowa. He married Mary Jane Timms, daughter of Richard Timms and Elizabeth Bibbee on 21 May 1861 in Wood County, Virginia. She was born on 18 Jan 1836 in Virginia. She died on 16 Jun 1917 in Vinton County, Ohio.

       More About Charles Wesley Barnett:
       Burial: Elk Cemetery, McArthur, Ohio

       More About Mary Jane Timms:
       Burial: Elk Cemetery, McArthur, Ohio


    iii.    Margaret Barnett, daughter of George William Barnett and Sarah Rockhold was born about 1836 in Virginia.

    iv.    George Washington Barnett, son of George William Barnett and Sarah Rockhold was born on 16 Feb 1840 in Wood County, Virginia. He died on 22 Oct 1910 in Wood County, West Virginia. He married Mary Elizabeth Taylor, daughter of William Henry Taylor and Catherine Selecman on 10 Oct 1864 in Wood County, West Virginia. She was born on 16 Apr 1846 in Wood County, Virginia. She died on 21

Nov 1914 in Parkersburg, West Virginia.

    v.    William Arthur Barnett, son of George William Barnett and Sarah Rockhold was born in Mar 1843 in Wood County, Virginia. He died on 16 Feb 1920 in Wood County, West Virginia. He married Ann Caroline Kincheloe, daughter of Daniel Kincheloe and Lodemia Truman Hill on 27 Oct 1868 in Wood County, West Virginia. She was born on 27 Oct 1845 in Wood County, Virginia. She died on 05 Jan 1928 in Wood County, West Virginia.

More About William Arthur Barnett:
Burial: Mt. Zion Cemetery, Wood County, West Virginia

9.    vi. Susan Minerva Barnett, daughter of George William Barnett and Sarah Rockhold was born on 28 Nov 1845 in Wood County, Virginia. She died on 15 Feb 1922 in Columbus, Ohio. She married Ezra Quimby Timms, son of Richard Timms and Elizabeth Bibbee on 26 Oct 1865 in Wood County, West Virginia. He was born on 19 Sep 1842 in Wirt County, Virginia. He died on 15 Aug 1925 in Clinton Township, Vinton County, Ohio.

20.    **Harrison Martin**.  He married **(unknown)**.

21.    **(unknown)**.

(unknown) and Harrison Martin had the following child:

10.    i. Albert Martin, son of Harrison Martin and (unknown) was born on 06 Jun 1867 in Virginia. He died on 15 Mar 1935 in Clinton, Vinton County, Ohio. He married Mary Alice (unknown).

24.    **William J. Pierce**, son of William Pierce and Jane Smith was born on 05 May 1815 in Ohio. He died on 12 Jul 1873 in Radcliff, Vinton County, Ohio. He married **Hannah Gregory** on 24 Apr 1847 in Jackson County, Ohio.

25.    **Hannah Gregory** was born in Jan 1829 in Ohio. She died on 17 Oct 1903 in Radcliff, Vinton County, Ohio.

More About William J.
Pierce:
Cause Of Death: Stroke
Occupation: Farmer

Hannah Gregory and William J. Pierce had the following children:

    i.    Jane Pierce, daughter of William J. Pierce and Hannah Gregory was born on 10 Apr 1848 in Vinton County, Ohio. She died on 30 Mar 1942 in Clinton, Vinton County, Ohio.

    ii.   Frances Pierce, daughter of William J. Pierce and Hannah Gregory was born in 1849 in Vinton County, Ohio. She died in 1932.

    iii.  Jaspur Pierce, son of William J. Pierce and Hannah Gregory was born on 24 Jan 1851 in Vinton County, Ohio. He died on 20 Aug 1931 in Vinton, Vinton County, Ohjo.

More About Jaspur Pierce:
Burial: 22 Jul 1931 in Radcliff Cemetery, Vinton County,
Ohio Cause Of Death: ; Automobile Accident

iv.   Mary Ellen Pierce, daughter of William J. Pierce and Hannah Gregory was born in 1853.

v.   Harvey Pierce, son of William J. Pierce and Hannah Gregory was born on 09 Jan 1854. He died on 27 May 1931 in Vinton Township, Vinton County, Ohio. He married Lydia (unknown). She died after 27 May 1931.

More About Harvey Pierce:
Burial: 30 May 1931 in Radcliff, Vinton County,
Ohio Cause Of Death: ; Cerebral Hemorrhage
Occupation: ; Farmer

12.   vi. Pinkney Pierce, son of William J. Pierce and Hannah Gregory was born on 03 Oct 1855 in Radcliff, Vinton County, Ohio. He died on 17 Dec 1936 in Gallipolis, Ohio. He married Malinda Gold on 06 Feb 1879 in Vinton County, Ohio. She was born on 05 Dec 1857 in Radcliff, Vinton County, Ohio. She died on 17 Oct 1943 in Vinton County, Ohio. He married Mary (unknown).

vii.   Harry Pierce, son of William J. Pierce and Hannah Gregory was born in 1856.

viii.   Issac Pierce, son of William J. Pierce and Hannah Gregory was born in 1859 in Vinton County, Ohio. He died on 09 Apr 1890 in Vinton Township, Vinton County, Ohio. He married Jane Lowe on 22 Aug 1881 in Vinton County, Ohio.

More About Issac Pierce:
Occupation:  Farmer

ix.   Gilruth Pierce, son of William J. Pierce and Hannah Gregory was born on 05 Jan 1859 in Vinton County, Ohio. He died on 26 Mar 1938 in Clinton Township, Vinton County, Ohio. He married Emma Swises.

x.   Mahala Catherine Pierce, daughter of William J. Pierce and Hannah Gregory was born on 19 Mar 1865 in Vinton County, Ohio. She died on 07 Jul 1942 in Radcliff, Vinton County, Ohio.

xi.   Caroline Pierce, daughter of William J. Pierce and Hannah Gregory was born on 04 Mar 1868 in Vinton County, Ohio. She died on 28 Jun 1941 in Vinton Township, Vinton County, Ohio. She married John Riley on 12 Sep 1882 in Vinton County, Ohio.

More About Caroline Pierce:
Burial:  01 Jul 1941 in Radcliff, Vinton County,
Ohio Cause Of Death: Aortic Insufficiency


28.   **Louis Castor**.  He married **Melvina Martin**.

29.   **Melvina Martin**.

Melvina Martin and Louis Castor had the following child:
14.   i. Elias Charles Castor, son of Louis Castor and Melvina Martin was born on 25 Jan 1871 in Meigs County, Ohio. He died on 30 Sep 1952 in Elk Township, Vinton County, Ohio. He married Loveta Eakin, daughter of Joseph Eakin and Hulda Lane on 26 May 1894 in Vinton County, Ohio. She was born in Jul 1876 in July Ohio. She died on 14 Mar 1916 in Elk Township, Vinton County, Ohio.

30. **Joseph Eakin**. He married **Hulda Lane**.

31. **Hulda Lane**.

Hulda Lane and Joseph Eakin had the following child:

15.      i. Loveta Eakin, daughter of Joseph Eakin and Hulda Lane was born in Jul 1876 in July Ohio. She died on 14 Mar 1916 in Elk Township, Vinton County, Ohio. She married Elias Charles Castor, son of Louis Castor and Melvina Martin on 26 May 1894 in Vinton County, Ohio. He was born on 25 Jan 1871 in Meigs County, Ohio. He died on 30 Sep 1952 in Elk Township, Vinton County, Ohio.

### Generation 6

32. **John B. Timms** was born on 31 Jan 1776 in Virginia. He died on 10 Oct 1843 in Wirt County, Virginia. He married **Nancy Davis** on 03 Apr 1803 in Loudoun County, Virginia.

33. **Nancy Davis** was born on 13 Feb 1779 in Maryland. She died on 16 Mar 1872 in Vinton County, Ohio.


More About Nancy Davis:
Burial: Elk Cemetery, McArthur, Ohio

Nancy Davis and John B. Timms had the following children:

16.      i. Richard Timms, son of John B. Timms and Nancy Davis was born on 13 Jan 1804 in Loudoun County, Virginia. He died on 16 Oct 1878 in Dundas, Vinton County, Ohio. He married Elizabeth Bibbee, daughter of John E. Bibbee and Elizabeth Spaecht on 01 Nov 1832 in Wood County, Virginia. She was born on 21 Nov 1805 in Wood County, Virginia. She died on 25 Mar 1879 in Dundas, Ohio.

     ii. Margaret Timms, daughter of John B. Timms and Nancy Davis was born on 28 Sep 1805 in Virginia. She married (unknown) Bayliss. She married John McFarland on 06 Mar 1828 in Wood County, Virginia. She married Caleb Wiseman on 18 Jan 1851 in Wirt County, Virginia.

     iii. William D. Timms, son of John B. Timms and Nancy Davis was born on 07 Jan 1809 in Wirt County, Virginia. He died on 30 Apr 1867 in Wirt County, West Virginia. He married Britannia Jane Saunders on 06 Dec 1840 in Wood County, Virginia. She was born in 1815. She died in 1882.

     iv. Jesse Timms, son of John B. Timms and Nancy Davis was born on 30 May 1810 in Virginia. He died on 25 Apr 1868. He married Mary Ann McCown on 21 Aug 1838. She was born in 1820. She died in 1895.

     v. James Timms, son of John B. Timms and Nancy Davis was born on 14 Mar 1812 in Virginia. He married Jane Marsh on 18 Aug 1838.

     vi. Mary Rose Timms, daughter of John B. Timms and Nancy Davis was born on 13 Feb 1815 in Virginia. She married Lewis C. Coe on 22 Jun 1847.

     vii. Elisha Timms, child of John B. Timms and Nancy Davis was born on 27 Jan 1818 in Virginia. Elisha married Jane E. Cheatain on 17 Jul 1841.

34. **John E. Bibbee**, son of John Bibbee and Susannah (unknown) was born on 08 Jan 1772 in Delaware. He died on 02 May 1828 in Leachtown, Virginia. He married **Elizabeth Spaecht** on 23 Apr 1802 in Wood County, Virginia.

35. **Elizabeth Spaecht** was born on 05 Mar 1781 in Pennsylvania. She died on 11 Oct 1845 in

Leachtown, Virginia.


More About John E. Bibbee:
Burial: Bibbee Cemetery, Leachtown, Virginia
Occupation: Farmer


More About Elizabeth Spaecht:
Burial: Bibbee Cemetery, Leachtown, Virginia

Elizabeth Spaecht and John E. Bibbee had the following children:

17.      i. Elizabeth Bibbee, daughter of John E. Bibbee and Elizabeth Spaecht was born on 21 Nov 1805 in Wood County, Virginia. She died on 25 Mar 1879 in Dundas, Ohio. She married Richard Timms, son of John B. Timms and Nancy Davis on 01 Nov 1832 in Wood County, Virginia. He was born on 13 Jan 1804 in Loudoun County, Virginia. He died on 16 Oct 1878 in Dundas, Vinton County, Ohio.

      ii. Mary Bibbee, daughter of John E. Bibbee and Elizabeth Spaecht was born on 24 Jun 1806 in Wood County, Virginia. She died on 08 Jul 1876 in Wood County, West Virginia. She married George Page on 08 Apr 1832 in Wood County, Virginia. He was born on 07 Nov 1808 in Wood County, Virginia. He died on 08 Aug 1893 in Wood County, West Virginia.

      iii. Susan Bibbee, daughter of John E. Bibbee and Elizabeth Spaecht was born on 23 Oct 1807 in Wood County, Virginia. She died on 06 Jun 1883 in Wood County, West Virginia. She married John Page, son of Robert H. Page and Frances V. Leach on 08 Mar 1842 in Wood County, Virginia. He was born on 19 Nov 1804 in Virginia. He died on 07 Feb 1896 in Wood County, West Virginia.

      iv. Charles Bibbee, son of John E. Bibbee and Elizabeth Spaecht was born on 29 Mar 1809 in Wood County, Virginia. He died on 02 May 1882 in Wood County, West Virginia. He married Adaline Hutchinson, daughter of Oliver Hutchinson and Sarah Page on 30 Oct 1834 in Wood County, Virginia. She was born on 30 Oct 1813 in Wood County, Virginia. She died on 27 Apr 1869 in Wood County, West Virginia.

      v. Lucinda Bibbee, daughter of John E. Bibbee and Elizabeth Spaecht was born on 08 Nov 1810 in Wood County, Virginia. She died on 11 Aug 1868 in Wood County, West Virginia.

      vi. Eveline Bibbee, daughter of John E. Bibbee and Elizabeth Spaecht was born on 13 Oct 1812 in Wood County, Virginia. She died on 21 Aug 1895 in Leachtown, West Virginia.

      vii. John E. Bibbee, son of John E. Bibbee and Elizabeth Spaecht was born on 21 Oct 1814 in Wood County, Virginia. He died on 22 May 1882 in Wood County, West Virginia. He married Permelia Ann Barnett on 23 Apr 1850 in Wood County, Virginia. She was born on 16 Aug 1829 in Wood County, Virginia. She died on 07 Dec 1916 in Leachtown, West Virginia.

      viii. Emily Bibbee, daughter of John E. Bibbee and Elizabeth Spaecht was born on 11 Jul 1816 in Wood County, Virginia. She died on 19 Jan 1832 in Leachtown, Virginia.

      ix. Jeptha W. Bibbee, son of John E. Bibbee and Elizabeth Spaecht was born on 31 Aug 1818 in Leachtown, Virginia. He died on 18 Aug 1896 in Wood County, West Virginia. He married Elily Catherine Hannaman on 01 Jun 1847 in Wood County, Virginia. She was born on 12 Dec 1825 in Wood County, Virginia. She died on 26 Oct 1848 in Wood County, Virginia. He married Eleanor Rosella Butcher on 28 Jan

1850 in Wood County, Virginia. She was born on 23 Nov 1824 in Randolf County, Virginia. She died on 06 Nov 1905 in Wood County, West Virginia.

    x.   Sarah Ann Bibbee, daughter of John E. Bibbee and Elizabeth Spaecht was born on 15 Jan 1821 in Wood County, Virginia. She died on 01 May 1897 in Wood County, West Virginia.

    xi.   Frances Jane Bibbee, daughter of John E. Bibbee and Elizabeth Spaecht was born on 15 Apr 1823 in Wood County, Virginia. She died on 11 Aug 1895 in Wood County, West Virginia.

    xii.   Caroline M. T. Bibbee, daughter of John E. Bibbee and Elizabeth Spaecht was born on 02 Jun 1827 in Wood County, Virginia. She died on 20 Jul 1876 in Wood County, West Virginia.

38.    **Charles Rockhold**.  He married **Permelia Wright**.

39.    **Permelia Wright**.

Permelia Wright and Charles Rockhold had the following child:

19.    i.   Sarah Rockhold, daughter of Charles Rockhold and Permelia Wright was born on 26 Feb 1802 in Wirt County, Virginia. She died on 03 Oct 1890. She married George William Barnett on 02 Oct 1828 in Wood County, Virginia. He was born on 17 Jun 1803 in Wood County, Virginia. He died on 29 Aug 1885 in Wood County, West Virginia.

48.    **William Pierce**, son of Richard Pierce and Margaret Knight was born on 22 Jan 1787 in Montgomery County, Virginia. He died on 28 Feb 1870 in Radcliff, Vinton County, Ohio. He married **Jane Smith** on 29 Oct 1811.

49.    **Jane Smith** was born on 26 Jan 1791 in Montgomery County, Virginia. She died on 12 Jul 1874 in Radcliff, Vinton County, Ohio.


More About William Pierce:
Burial: Radcliff Cemetery, Vinton County, Ohio
Military Service:  Ohio Militia, War of 1812


More About Jane Smith:
Burial: Radcliff Cemetery, Vinton County, Ohio


Notes for Jane Smith:
Death certificate of Samuel Pierce gives Jane Wright for his mother's name.

Jane Smith and William Pierce had the following children:

24.    i.   William J. Pierce, son of William Pierce and Jane Smith was born on 05 May 1815 in Ohio. He died on 12 Jul 1873 in Radcliff, Vinton County, Ohio. He married Hannah Gregory on 24 Apr 1847 in Jackson County, Ohio. She was born in Jan 1829 in Ohio. She died on 17 Oct 1903 in Radcliff, Vinton County, Ohio.

    ii.   John S. Pierce, son of William Pierce and Jane Smith was born in 1817. He married Nancy Arbaugh.

    iii.   James Pierce, son of William Pierce and Jane Smith was born in 1821. He died on 29 Apr 1896 in Radcliff, Vinton County, Ohio.

iv.	Gilruth Pierce, son of William Pierce and Jane Smith was born on 26 Mar 1824. He died on 21 Sep 1908 in Decatur County, Iowa. He married Eliza Ann Walden, daughter of William Walden and Emily Wilson on 30 Dec 1852 in Vinton County, Ohio. She was born about 1836 in Ohio.

v.	Thomas Pierce, son of William Pierce and Jane Smith was born in 1827.

vi.	Marcus Pierce, son of William Pierce and Jane Smith was born in 1828.

vii.	Samuel Pierce, son of William Pierce and Jane Smith was born on 12 Mar 1828. He died on 16 May 1912 in Zaleski, Ohio.

More About Samuel Pierce:
Burial: 17 Mar 1912 in Radcliff Cemetery, Vinton County,
Ohio Occupation: ; Farmer

viii.	Wesley Pierce, son of William Pierce and Jane Smith was born in Mar 1831 in Ohio. He died on 23 Jan 1917 in Vinton, Vinton County, Ohio. He married Catherine (unknown). She was born in Sep 1835 in Ohio.

More About Wesley Pierce:
Burial: 26 Jan 1917 in Radcliff Cemetery, Vinton County, Ohio

ix.	Jane Pierce, daughter of William Pierce and Jane Smith was born in 1833. She married Joseph Arbaugh.

x.	Isabella Pierce, daughter of William Pierce and Jane Smith was born in 1836. She married Leonard Arbaugh.

xi.	Sarah Ann Pierce, daughter of William Pierce and Jane Smith was born in 1838.

---

**Generation 7**

68.	**John Bibbee** was born on 04 Jun 1736 in Delaware. He died on 21 Jun 1817 in Apple Grove, Meigs County, Ohio. He married **Susannah (unknown)**.

69.	**Susannah (unknown)** was born on 26 Oct 1744 in Wood County, Virginia. She died on 16 Jul 1828 in Apple Grove, Meigs County, Ohio.


More About John Bibbee:
Burial: Bibbee Cemetery, Meigs County, Ohio


More About Susannah (unknown):
Burial: Bibbee Cemetery, Meigs County, Ohio

Susannah (unknown) and John Bibbee had the following children:
i.	William Bibbee, son of John Bibbee and Susannah (unknown) was born on 24 Nov 1766 in Wood County, Virginia. He died on 25 Apr 1842 in Jackson County, Virginia. He married Deborah Hughes on 07 Jan 1795 in Harrison County, Virginia. She was born about 1775 in Hackers Creek, Virginia.

ii.	Susanna Bibbee, daughter of John Bibbee and Susannah (unknown) was born on 28 Jul 1769 in Maryland. She died on 02 Apr 1842 in Knox County, Illinois. She married John Henry Hannaman, son of Christopher Hannaman and Mary O'Neal on 15 Feb 1787 in Harrison County, Virginia. He was born on 15 Feb 1760 in Otsego County, New York. He died on 15 Nov 1832 in Livingston County, New York.

34. iii. John E. Bibbee, son of John Bibbee and Susannah (unknown) was born on 08 Jan 1772 in Delaware. He died on 02 May 1828 in Leachtown, Virginia. He married Elizabeth Spaecht on 23 Apr 1802 in Wood County, Virginia. She was born on 05 Mar 1781 in Pennsylvania. She died on 11 Oct 1845 in Leachtown, Virginia.

iv. Rachel Bibbee, daughter of John Bibbee and Susannah (unknown) was born on 04 Mar 1774 in Maryland. She died on 11 Jul 1856 in Clark County, Ohio. She married Jacob B. Ellsworth, son of Jacob b. Ellsworth and Hannah Bennett on 10 Apr 1793 in Harrison County, Virginia. He was born on 24 Apr 1775 in Augusta County, Virginia. He died on 23 Oct 1865 in Clark County, Ohio.

v. Isaac Bibbee, son of John Bibbee and Susannah (unknown) was born on 28 Mar 1776 in Wood County, Virginia. He married Cynthia Lee. She was born about 1786 in Virginia.

vi. Elizabeth Bibbee, daughter of John Bibbee and Susannah (unknown) was born on 4 Aug 1778 in Wood County, Virginia. She died on 09 Jan 1856 in Ravenswood, Virginia. She married Andrew S. Flesher, son of Henry Weston Flesher and Elizabeth Bush on 21 Feb 1793 in Harrison County, Virginia. He was born on 01 May 1771 in Hampshire County, Virginia. He died on 14 Oct 1850 in Ravenswood, Virginia.

vii. Abraham Bibbee, son of John Bibbee and Susannah (unknown) was born on 08 Feb 1780.

viii. Joseph Bibbee, son of John Bibbee and Susannah (unknown) was born on 05 Apr 1783 in Virginia. He died on 08 Aug 1855 in Jackson County, Virginia. He married Margaret Parsons on 02 Aug 1809 in Gallia County, Ohio. She was born about 1788 in Harrison County, Virginia. She died about 1883.

ix. Rebecca Bibbee, daughter of John Bibbee and Susannah (unknown) was born on 24 Nov 1786.

x. Elijah Bibbee, son of John Bibbee and Susannah (unknown) was born on 23 Dec 1789.

96. **Richard Pierce**, son of Ephraim Pierce and Mary Stevenson was born on 01 Jan 1733. He died in Jan 1821 in Montgomery County, Virginia. He married **Margaret Knight** in 1773.

97. **Margaret Knight**.

Margaret Knight and Richard Pierce had the following children:
i. Abigail Pierce.

ii. Phoebe Pierce, daughter of Richard Pierce and Margaret Knight was born in Montgomery County, Virginia. She married James Thompson.

iii. Samuel Pierce, son of Richard Pierce and Margaret Knight was born about 1779. He married Mary Page.

iv. Freelove Pierce, daughter of Richard Pierce and Margaret Knight was born in 1781. She married David Smith.

v. Jonathan Pierce, son of Richard Pierce and Margaret Knight was born in 1783. He died on 01 Jan 1864.

48. vi. William Pierce, son of Richard Pierce and Margaret Knight was born on 22 Jan 1787 in Montgomery County, Virginia. He died on 28 Feb 1870 in Radcliff, Vinton County, Ohio. He married Jane Smith on 29 Oct 1811. She was born on 26 Jan 1791 in Montgomery County, Virginia. She died on 12 Jul 1874 in Radcliff, Vinton County, Ohio.

vii. Thomas Pierce, son of Richard Pierce and Margaret Knight was born about 1789. He married Mary Muirhead.

viii. Richard Pierce, son of Richard Pierce and Margaret Knight was born about 1791.

ix. Sarah Pierce, daughter of Richard Pierce and Margaret Knight was born on 11 Jun 1797. She married John Garlick.

## Generation 8

192. **Ephraim Pierce**, son of Mial Pierce and Judith Rounds was born on 09 Nov 1712 in Swansea, Massachusetts. He married **Mary Stevenson**.

193. **Mary Stevenson**.

Mary Stevenson and Ephraim Pierce had the following children:

96. i. Richard Pierce, son of Ephraim Pierce and Mary Stevenson was born on 01 Jan 1733. He died in Jan 1821 in Montgomery County, Virginia. He married Margaret Knight in 1773.

ii. Clother Pierce, son of Ephraim Pierce and Mary Stevenson was born on 24 May 1738.

iii. Peleg Pierce, son of Ephraim Pierce and Mary Stevenson was born on 13 Jan 1741.

iv. Mary Pierce, daughter of Ephraim Pierce and Mary Stevenson was born on 27 Aug 1745.

## Generation 9

384. **Mial Pierce** was born on 24 Apr 1693 in Rehoboth, Massachusetts. He died on 18 Oct 1786 in Warwick, Rhode Island. He married **Judith Rounds** on 26 Nov 1711 in Swansea, Mass..

385. **Judith Rounds** was born about 1687 in Swansea, Massachusetts. She died on 06 Oct 1744 in Rehoboth, Mass..

Judith Rounds and Mial Pierce had the following children:

i. Caleb Pierce.

ii. Judith Pierce.

193. iii. Ephraim Pierce, son of Mial Pierce and Judith Rounds was born on 09 Nov 1712 in Swansea, Massachusetts. He married Mary Stevenson.

iv. Wheeler Pierce, son of Mial Pierce and Judith Rounds was born on 01 Jul 1714.

v. Nathan Pierce, son of Mial Pierce and Judith Rounds was born on 12 Feb 1715.

vi.   Mary Pierce, daughter of Mial Pierce and Judith Rounds was born on 16 Oct 1718.

vii.   Mial Pierce, son of Mial Pierce and Judith Rounds was born on 24 Mar 1720.

## Generation 1

1. **JOHN B.**[1] **TIMMS** was born on 31 Jan 1776 in Virginia. He died on 10 Oct 1843 in Wirt County, Virginia. He married Nancy Davis on 03 Apr 1803 in Loudoun County, Virginia. She was born on 13 Feb 1779 in Maryland. She died on 16 Mar 1872 in Vinton County, Ohio.

   More About Nancy Davis:
   Burial: Elk Cemetery, McArthur, Ohio

   John B. Timms and Nancy Davis had the following children:

   i. RICHARD[2] TIMMS was born on 13 Jan 1804 in Loudoun County, Virginia. He died on 16 Oct 1878 in Dundas, Vinton County, Ohio. He married Elizabeth Bibbee, daughter of John E. Bibbee and Elizabeth Spaecht on 01 Nov 1832 in Wood County, Virginia. She was born on 21 Nov 1805 in Wood County, Virginia. She died on 25 Mar 1879 in Dundas, Ohio.

   MARGARET TIMMS was born on 28 Sep 1805 in Virginia. She married (UNKNOWN) BAYLISS. She married (2) JOHN MCFARLAND on 06 Mar 1828 in Wood County, Virginia. She married (3) CALEB WISEMAN on 18 Jan 1851 in Wirt County, Virginia.

   iii. WILLIAM D. TIMMS was born on 07 Jan 1809 in Wirt County, Virginia. He died on 30 Apr 1867 in Wirt County, West Virginia. He married Britannia Jane Saunders on 06 Dec 1840 in Wood County, Virginia. She was born in 1815. She died in 1882.

   iv. JESSE TIMMS was born on 30 May 1810 in Virginia. He died on 25 Apr 1868. He married Mary Ann McCown on 21 Aug 1838. She was born in 1820. She died in 1895.

   v. JAMES TIMMS was born on 14 Mar 1812 in Virginia. He married Jane Marsh on 18 Aug 1838.

   vi. MARY ROSE TIMMS was born on 13 Feb 1815 in Virginia. She married Lewis C. Coe on 22 Jun 1847.

   vii. ELISHA TIMMS was born on 27 Jan 1818 in Virginia. Elisha married Jane E. Cheatain on 17 Jul 1841.

## Generation 2

2. **RICHARD**[2] **TIMMS** (John B.[1]) was born on 13 Jan 1804 in Loudoun County, Virginia. He died on 16 Oct 1878 in Dundas, Vinton County, Ohio. He married Elizabeth Bibbee, daughter of John E. Bibbee and Elizabeth Spaecht on 01 Nov 1832 in Wood County, Virginia. She was born on 21 Nov 1805 in Wood County, Virginia. She died on 25 Mar 1879 in Dundas, Ohio.

   More About Richard Timms:
   Burial: Elk Cemetery, McArthur, Ohio
   Occupation: Innkeeper
   Occupation: Farmer

   More About Elizabeth Bibbee: Burial:
   Elk Cemetery, McArthur, Ohio

   Notes for Elizabeth Bibbee:
   "TIMMS- Elizabeth Timms, wife of the late Richard Timms, was born in Wood County, West

Virginia November 21, 1805 and died at McArthur Station ,Vinton County Ohio on March 25th, 1879. In the 74th years of her age. She united with the M.E. Church when young and lived a faithful and true Christian to the end. For five years she had been an invalid. During three years her afflictions were many and great; but through all, she bore up with marked patience, never once having been heard to complain. In their many afflictions, this much afflicted family have the sympathies of many friends.

And may the members of this family who yet remain, emulate the spirit of their sainted mother and like her through the grace of our Lord Jesus Christ, receive a crown of eternal life. JCA."


Richard Timms and Elizabeth Bibbee had the following children:

4.  i. HARRIET L.[3] TIMMS was born on 17 Sep 1833 in Virginia. She died on 18 Nov 1865 in West Virginia. She married James William Morehead, son of Nathaniel H. Morehead and Mary Richards on 12 Dec 1856 in Virginia. He was born in May 1826 in Wood County, Virginia. He died in 1909.

5.  ii. MARY JANE TIMMS was born on 18 Jan 1836 in Virginia. She died on 16 Jun 1917 in Vinton County, Ohio. She married Charles Wesley Barnett, son of George William Barnett and Sarah Rockhold on 21 May 1861 in Wood County, Virginia. He was born on 16 Feb 1834 in Wood County, Virginia. He died on 06 Jun 1903 in Oskaloosa, Iowa.

6.  iii. JOHN BIBBEE TIMMS was born on 18 Feb 1838 in Wirt County, Virginia. He died on 2  Oct 1911 in Clinton, Vinton County, Ohio. He married Roseanna Barnes, daughter of John Barnes and Frances Davis on 24 Sep 1863 in Wirt County, West Virginia. She was born on 30 Apr 1844 in Wirt County, Virginia. She died on 15 Apr 1927 in Vinton County, Ohio.

7.  iv. CHARLES W. TIMMS was born on 19 Dec 1839 in Wirt County, Virginia. He died on 4  Nov 1906 in Dundas, Vinton County, Ohio. He married Charlotte Elizabeth Dowd, daughter of John Dowd and Olive Fuller on 11 Oct 1877 in McArthur, Vinton County, Ohio. She was born on 17 Jan 1857 in Vinton County, Ohio. She died on 12 Dec 1934 in Vinton County, Ohio.

  v. EZRA QUIMBY TIMMS was born on 19 Sep 1842 in Wirt County, Virginia. He died on Aug 1925 in Clinton Township, Vinton County, Ohio. He married Susan Minerva Barnett, daughter of George William Barnett and Sarah Rockhold on 26 Oct 1865 in Wood County, West Virginia. She was born on 28 Nov 1845 in Wood County, Virginia. She died on 15 Feb 1922 in Columbus, Ohio.

  vi. SARAH MARGARET TIMMS was born on 15 May 1844 in Wirt County, Virginia. She died on 23 Dec 1921 in Mahaska County, Iowa. She married Joseph Harvey Evans, son of Jacob Evans and Mary (unknown) on 25 Nov 1886 in Mahaska County, Iowa. He was born on 10 Aug 1822 in Maryland. He died on 09 Jul 1908 in Oskaloosa, Mahaska County, Iowa.

  vii. FRANCES B. TIMMS was born on 08 Jun 1848 in Virginia. She died in 1920 in Long Beach, California. She married William S. England on 24 Mar 1869 in Vinton County, Ohio.


3. **WILLIAM D.[2] TIMMS** (John B.[1]) was born on 07 Jan 1809 in Wirt County, Virginia. He died on 30 Apr 1867 in Wirt County, West Virginia. He married Britannia Jane Saunders on 06 Dec 1840 in Wood County, Virginia. She was born in 1815. She died in 1882.

William D. Timms and Britannia Jane Saunders had the following children:

1    MARY FRANCIS[3] TIMMS.  She died in 1924.

2    MARGARET JANE TIMMS was born in 1844. She died in 1933.

3    CLARA PERMILLIA TIMMS was born in 1848. She died in 1934.

---

**Generation 3**

4.    **HARRIET L.**[3] **TIMMS** (Richard[2], John B.[1]) was born on 17 Sep 1833 in Virginia. She died on 18 Nov 1865 in West Virginia. She married James William Morehead, son of Nathaniel H. Morehead and Mary Richards on 12 Dec 1856 in Virginia. He was born in May 1826 in Wood County, Virginia. He died in 1909.

James William Morehead and Harriet L. Timms had the following children:

11.        i. EMMA L.[4] MOREHEAD was born on 09 Sep 1859 in Virginia. She died on 12 Apr 1922 in West Virginia. She married George W. Stephens on 19 May 1881 in Wirt County, West Virginia. He was born on 06 Jul 1852 in Virginia. He died on 21 Sep 1916 in West Virginia.

12.        ii. CHARLES ANDREW MOREHEAD was born in Oct 1860 in Wirt County, Virginia. He married (1) JOSEPHINE DEEM on 08 Oct 1885 in Wood County, West Virginia. She was born in Apr 1867 in Wood County, West Virginia. He married (2) LULU MAY ROBERTS on 12 Feb 1919 in Wood County, West Virginia. She was born about 1867 in Wirt County, West Virginia. She died in 1928.

5.    **MARY JANE**[3] **TIMMS** (Richard[2], John B.[1]) was born on 18 Jan 1836 in Virginia. She died on 16 Jun 1917 in Vinton County, Ohio. She married Charles Wesley Barnett, son of George William Barnett and Sarah Rockhold on 21 May 1861 in Wood County, Virginia. He was born on 16 Feb 1834 in Wood County, Virginia. He died on 06 Jun 1903 in Oskaloosa, Iowa.

More About Mary Jane Timms:
Burial: Elk Cemetery, McArthur, Ohio

More About Charles Wesley Barnett:
Burial: Elk Cemetery, McArthur, Ohio

Charles Wesley Barnett and Mary Jane Timms had the following children:

        i.    EMMA ELIZABETH[4] BARNETT was born on 07 Aug 1862. She died on 06 Apr 1890.

13.        ii.    RHODA ISABELLA BARNETT was born on 13 Feb 1866 in Dundas, Ohio. She died on 4  Nov 1957 in Mahaska County, Iowa. She married Calvin W. Woodruff on 23 Oct 1889 in Vinton County, Ohio. He was born on 02 Apr 1837 in Muskingum County, ohio. He died in 1916.

14.        iii.    BENJAMIN FRANKLIN BARNETT was born on 30 Apr 1868 in Vinton County, Ohio. He died on 10 Jun 1949 in Stockton, California. He married Malinda Louella Adair on Nov 1904 in Mahaska County, Iowa. She was born on 26 Mar 1887 in Mahaska County, Iowa. She died on 04 Jan 1954 in Stockton, California.

        iv.    SARAH MARGARET BARNETT was born on 29 Nov 1869 in Vinton County, Ohio. She died on 16 Oct 1871 in Vinton County, Ohio.

15.        v.    ANNA LAURIE BARNETT was born on 14 Jul 1873 in Vinton County, Ohio. She died on

---

04 Aug 1959 in Vinton County, Ohio. She married George E. Pugh on 02 Aug 1891 in Vinton County, Ohio. He was born on 13 Oct 1861 in Gallipolis Ferry, West Virginia. He died on 10 Sep 1959 in Vinton County, Ohio.

6.   **JOHN BIBBEE**[3] **TIMMS** (Richard[2], John B.[1]) was born on 18 Feb 1838 in Wirt County, Virginia. He died on 02 Oct 1911 in Clinton, Vinton County, Ohio. He married Roseanna Barnes, daughter of John Barnes and Frances Davis on 24 Sep 1863 in Wirt County, West Virginia. She was born on 30 Apr 1844 in Wirt County, Virginia. She died on 15 Apr 1927 in Vinton County, Ohio.

More About John Bibbee Timms:
Burial: Elk Cemetery, McArthur, Ohio
Cause Of Death: Muscular Rheumatism
Living In: 1880  Clinton, Vinton County, Ohio
Occupation:  Farmer

More About Roseanna Barnes:
Burial: 17 Apr 1927 in Elk Cemetery, McArthur, Ohio

John Bibbee Timms and Roseanna Barnes had the following children:

      i.    ANNIE E.[4] TIMMS was born about 1865 in Wirt County, West Virginia.

      ii.    HASELTON TIMMS was born on 04 Jul 1868 in Wirt County, West Virginia. She died on 20 Oct 1880 in Vinton County, Ohio.

16.    iii. MINNIE VICTORIA TIMMS was born on 21 Jan 1871 in Wirt County, West Virginia. She died on 11 Sep 1961 in Worthington, Ohio. She married Edward Warren Salts, son of George Salts and Mary Jane McKibbon on 18 Oct 1892 in Vinton County, Ohio. He was born on 05 Jul 1868 in Clinton Township, Vinton County, Ohio. He died on 2   Jan 1943 in Orange Township, Delaware County, Ohio.

      v.    EVALINA TIMMS was born about 1874 in Wirt County, West Virginia.

17.    v.    JOHN FRANKLIN TIMMS was born on 11 Oct 1879 in Vinton County, Ohio. He died on 4   Apr 1945 in Vinton County, Ohio. He married ELIZABETH AUSTIN. She was born about 1883 in Vinton County, Ohio. She died on 06 Jun 1955 in Vinton County, Ohio.

      vi.    CLARA A. TIMMS was born on 09 Nov 1882 in Vinton County, Ohio. She married Samuel F. Beckley on 29 Mar 1903 in Vinton County, Ohio. He was born on 06 Oct 1881 in Vinton County, Ohio.

7.   **CHARLES W.**[3] **TIMMS** (Richard[2], John B.[1]) was born on 19 Dec 1839 in Wirt County, Virginia. He died on 04 Nov 1906 in Dundas, Vinton County, Ohio. He married Charlotte Elizabeth Dowd, daughter of John Dowd and Olive Fuller on 11 Oct 1877 in McArthur, Vinton County, Ohio. She was born on 17 Jan 1857 in Vinton County, Ohio. She died on 12 Dec 1934 in Vinton County, Ohio.

More About Charles W. Timms:
Burial: 06 Nov 1906 in Elk Cemetery, McArthur, Ohio
Military Service: Bet. 15 Aug 1862-17 Jun 1865 ; Company F, 11th West Virginia Infantry, U.S.A. (Civil War)
Military Service: 11 Sep 1864; Promoted to Corporal in Company F, 11th West Virginia Infantry

Notes for Charles W. Timms:
SOURCE: Vinton County, Ohio Newspaper McArthur Democrat Enquirer November 8,
1906

"Charles W. Timms, an honorable citizen and brave soldier, died November 4, at his home in Dundas, aged 66 years, 10 months and 15 days. He was born in West Virginia and served three years as corporal of Company F of the 11th West Virginia Infantry, being at Cedar Creek and many other battles.

He has been a resident of Dundas for 41 years. He was married to Charlotte E. Dowd in 1877. He leaves a widow, two sons and a daughter, brother and sister and a host of relatives and friends, sincere mourners of his departure.

Funeral services took place at the home on November 6th conducted by Dr. Taylor. Old comrades carried him to his grave in Elk Cemetery. A very large concourse of people attended the services

-------------------------------------------------------------------------------------------------------------------

Enlisted in Company F, 11th West Virginia Infantry, U.S. Army, at Newark, Virginia on August 15th, 1862.
Mustered out of Company F, 11th West Virginia Infantry at Richmond, Virginia on June 17, 1865.

More About Charlotte Elizabeth Dowd:
Burial: Elk Cemetery, McArthur, Ohio

Charles W. Timms and Charlotte Elizabeth Dowd had the following children:
> i. MARY E LIZABETH [4] TIMMS was born on 10 May 1878 in Vinton County, Ohio. She married ED BAY.

> ii. CARL E. TIMMS was born on 11 Oct 1880 in Vinton County, Ohio. He died on 03 Oct 1881 in Vinton County, Ohio.

> iii. JOHN R. TIMMS was born on 08 Mar 1882 in Vinton County, Ohio. He died on 13 Mar 1886 in Vinton County, Ohio.

> iv. HOMER TIMMS was born on 07 Feb 1884 in Vinton County, Ohio. He died on 16 Oct 1980 in Columbus, Ohio. He married ETTA (UNKNOWN). She was born about 1882 in Ohio.

>> More About Homer Timms:
>> Occupation: 1918 ; Fireman on Hocking Valley Railroad

> v. EZRA DOWD TIMMS was born on 03 Mar 1893 in Vinton County, Ohio. He died in May 1968 in Tallmadge, Ohio.

8. **EZRA QUIMBY**[3] **TIMMS** (Richard[2], John B.[1]) was born on 19 Sep 1842 in Wirt County, Virginia. He died on 15 Aug 1925 in Clinton Township, Vinton County, Ohio. He married Susan Minerva Barnett, daughter of George William Barnett and Sarah Rockhold on 26 Oct 1865 in Wood County, West Virginia. She was born on 28 Nov 1845 in Wood County, Virginia. She died on 15 Feb 1922 in Columbus, Ohio.

More About Ezra Quimby Timms:
Burial: 16 Aug 1925 in Hixon Cemetery, Vinton County, Ohio
Living In: 1880 Clinton, Vinton County, Ohio

Occupation: ; Farmer
Military Service: Bet. 15 Aug 1862-17 Jun 1865 ; Company F, 11th West Virginia Infantry, U.S.A. (Civil War)
Military Service: 07 Sep 1864 ; Promoted to Sergeant in Company F, 11th West Virginia Infantry.


Notes for Ezra Quimby Timms:
SOURCE: Vinton County Newspaper McArthur Democrat Enquirer August 19, 1925 "Death of Ezra Q. Timms"

"Ezra Quimby Timms aged 82 years died at his home in Dundas, Ohio Sunday August 15, at 4 o'clock. He was a Civil War veteran, sergeant in Co K. 11th West Virginia Infantry, serving about three years until the end of the war. A couple of sketches as to his arduous and patriotic services during these trying times were published in this paper during the past year. He was a man of fine capacity, a successful farmer and raiser of fine livestock in which he took commendable pride and was universally respected for his sterling qualities as a man and citizen.

Surviving are the following named children, grandchildren, and great grand children; his daughter Mrs Amy Salts of Dundas, her daughter Lulu Smith of Marion: daughter Ina Workman of Dundas; daughter Sybil Timms at Home: Sons of Amy Salts: Roy, Kenneth and Earl Salts of Detroit; Otto of Portsmouth Robert and Garvin at Dundas; son Henry Timms his daughter Helen; his son James W. Timms, Dundas, his daughter Mrs Alta Perriner of Cleveland, her daughter Betty Jane daughter Annie Russell, wife of Sam Russell of Dundas, their daughter Nellie Dye wife of Roy Dye; son of Charles Timms, his son John and daughter Alice, Dundas, two children of his son George (deceased) Barnet Timms of Wellsburg, West Virginia and daughter Blanche Timms of Milwaukee, Wis., daughter Mrs Jennie Bay wife of Earl Bay, their children Virginia, Charlene, Robert and Julian Richard;

The great grandchildren of deceased are Ralph and Mary Smith children of Lulu Smith; Louise and Marie Workman, children of Ina Workman; Russell and Theresa Dye, children of Nellie Dye; Betty Jane Perriner before mentioned.
Ida daughter of Ezra Timms who was the wife of M.S. Cox has been deceased for a number of years.

The funeral was at 2 o'clock on Monday afternoon at the residence, Rev. O.J. Howearth of Nelsonville and Dr. Taylor of McArthur officiating. Burial in the Hixon cemetery near Dundas, P. Gaskill undertaker. The Pall bearers were members of the American Legion: Dr H.S. James, Herbert Hamilton, Eura Frazee, Fred Button, James Warren, F.E. Weinrich. The honorary pall bearers were Civil War Veterans: Dr. C.B. Taylor, Capt. D.H. Moore, V.R. Sprague, Richard Clements, John Glover, John Franklin and Robert Hayes."

OBITUARY

Ezra Quimby Timms born September 19,1842 died August 15, 1925 aged 82 years 10 months and 27 days.
Mr. Timms was the son of Richard and Elizabeth Timms was born in Wirt County Virginia, which is now West Virginia, spending his boyhood days among his native hills. Securing a district school education and training himself as a farmer. When 20 years old he enlisted in the 11th W. Va. Infantry in the Union Army. This regiment was assigned to special duty and helped to win the hard battles of Cedar Creek and Winchester.
Mr. Timms witnessed the dashing ride of that gallant Phil Sheridan in the Cedar Creek fight. At Petersburg the regiment was almost killed and wounded. Mr. Timms serving almost 3 years continuous duty and fighting was never wounded nor in a hospital. At Spencer in Roane County, Virginia he was

captured and paroled the next day and honorably discharged June 17, 1865. In the fall of 1865 his father sold the home place in Virginia and moved to Dundas and bought 452 acres of land where Dundas now stands. Mr. Timms father died October 1875, his mother in March 1876. In the meantime he had returned to his native county and state and married Susan M. Barnett on October 26, 1865 who died the 15th of February 1922. To them were born 8 children, 20 grandchildren, and 7 great grandchildren. The children were:

    Amy L., who married Willis G. Salts
    Anna L., who married Samuel Russel
    Geneva E., who married Earl Bay
    Ida B., who married M. S. Cox
    and the four sons Henry M., James W.,  Charles V. and George B.

    Mr Timms united with the Christian Church at Bethel August 10, 1894 and retained his membership until his death. To this community the people have lost a true and sincere friend and neighbor; a patriotic citizen. Faithful to his duty, his friends numbered by his large acquaintance all of whom testify to his noble character and splendid citizenship. We cherish the memory of E.Q. Timms because of his stainless record and the life he has lived among us.
    We cannot at this time bid farewell to Sergeant Timms without paying a tribute to his army record as he is the last one of the Civil War veterans in our neigborhood. "Soldier rest! thy warfare is o'er
Sleep the sleep that knows no breaking
Dream of battlefields no more,'
Days of danger, nights of waking, In
our isle's enchanted hall
Hands unseen they couch are strewing,
Fairy strains of music fall,
Every sense in slumber dewing. Sergeant
Timms, rest!  thy warfare is o'er, Dream of
fighting fields no more;
Morn of toil, nor night of waking."

"CARD OF THANKS"
"We, the children of E.Q. Timms feel grateful to the friends, neighbors, those who furnished flowers and music at the funeral of our father, and take this means of thanking all.
The Children"
****************************************************************************
SOURCE: Vinton County Newspaper McArthur Democrat Enquirer June 10, 1925

"Sergeant Ezra Q. Timms of Dundas, 11th West Virginia Infantry, Civil War was a pleasant caller in our office Monday. Mr. Timms still has a remarkable accurate memory of events which he came in contact during "The Great Unpleasantness". He thinks that he and John Franklin of McArthur, late of Co. F. 36th Ohio Inf. are the only Vinton County soldiers now living who were present at the surrender of LEe and his army at Appomattox, Virginia in April 1865. He says the Confederate soldiers appeared to be rejoiced that the war was over. At the surrender, they got a good feed from the Union soldiers. The "rebs" were so hungry and exhausted that they could not walk 50 yards without sitting down. There were men of all ages among them from 15 to 60 years old. They were without either money or provisions, and how they ever got to their distant homes has always remained a mystery  to Sergeant Timms.
He and Mr. Franklin were both present at the famous battle of Cedar Creek, October 19, 1864 when Sheridan rode furiously up to the field  from "Twenty

Miles Away". A prisoner taken later, told how General Jubal Early, the confederate commander took the defeat. After the battle he tried to halt the retreat of his forces at Fisher's Hill, a long ridge connecting Massanutten Mountain with North Mountain. He sat on his horse beseeching his troppst o half and form a line of defense. "Boys won't you rally once more for all Jubal?" "Nary a rally, Jubal" replied the discouraged troopers and so ended the fighting in the Shenandoah Valley."

----------------------------------------------------------------------------------------------------

Ezra Timms marriage record states he was born in Wood County, Virginia instead of Wirt County, Virginia.
----------------------------------------------------------------------------------------------------
Enlisted in Company F, 11th West Virginia Infantry, U.S. Army, at Newark, Virginia on August 15, 1862.
----------------------------------------------------------------------------------------------------
Mustered out of Company F, 11th West Virginia Infantry at Richmond, Virginia on June 17, 1865.
----------------------------------------------------------------------------------------------------


More About Susan Minerva Barnett:
Burial: 17 Feb 1922 in Hixon Cemetery, Vinton County, Ohio
Cause Of Death: Liver Cancer

Ezra Quimby Timms and Susan Minerva Barnett had the following children:

18.      i. AMY LOUISE[4] TIMMS was born on 24 Mar 1868 in Clinton Township, Vinton County, Ohio. She died on 04 May 1959 in Vinton County, Ohio. She married Willis Garvin Salts, son of John Salts and Ivy Hoffiner on 21 Jun 1888 in Vinton County, Ohio. He was born on 02 Mar 1863 in Vinton County, Ohio. He died on 10 Nov 1910 in Vinton County, Ohio.

19.      ii. HENRY MILTON TIMMS was born on 31 Mar 1870 in Dundas, Vinton County, Ohio. He died on 15 Feb 1953 in Wellston, Ohio. He married Anna Gunning, daughter of Orville Gunning and Catherine (unknown) on 29 Mar 1889. She was born on 23 Oct 1864 in Vinton County, Ohio. She died on 17 Jun 1943 in Clinton, Vinton County, Ohio.

20.      iii. JAMES W. TIMMS was born on 09 Mar 1872 In Clinton Township, Vinton County, Ohio. He died on 02 Mar 1961. He married Sarah J. Bobo, daughter of Thomas W. Bobo and Mary E. (unknown) on 30 Jan 1895 in Vinton County, Ohio. She was born about 1865 in Ohio.

21.      iv. ANNA LUELLA TIMMS was born on 23 Dec 1873 in Clinton Township, Vinton County, Ohio. She died on 02 Jan 1949 in Clinton Township, Vinton County, Ohio. She married Samuel Russell on 01 Jan 1896 in Vinton County, Ohio. He died after 02 Jan 1949.

22.      v. CHARLES VANCE TIMMS was born on 19 Dec 1875 in Vinton County, Ohio. He died on 01 Mar 1961 in Hocking County, Ohio. He married Maggie Elizabeth Martin, daughter of Albert Martin and Mary Alice (unknown) on 01 Jan 1918 in Vinton County, Ohio. She was born on 03 Jan 1889 in Vinton County, Ohio. She died on 17 Jan 1939 in Clinton, Vinton County, Ohio.

23.      vi. GEORGE BARNETT TIMMS was born on 29 Jul 1878 in Dundas, Clinton Township, Vinton County, Ohio. He died on 10 Sep 1916. He married (1) IRMA PIERCE on 06

Sep 1902. He married (2) SADIE WORTMAN on 17 Sep 1907 in Hamilton, Ohio. He married (3) SARAH E LIZABETH MONROE, daughter of Charles B. Monroe and Eliza Westcott on 17 Sep 1907 in Cincinnati, Ohio. She was born on 13 Feb 1878 in Tuscola, Illinois. She died on 07 Jul 1940.

    vii.    IDA BLANCHE TIMMS was born on 02 Aug 1883 in Dundas, Vinton County, Ohio. She died on 17 Jun 1915 in Los Angeles, California. She married Milton Shed Cox, son of James G. Cox and Nancy Graves on 24 Apr 1913 in Cincinnati, Ohio. He was born in 1868 in Vinton County, Ohio.

24.    viii. SUSAN GENEVA TIMMS was born on 04 Feb 1886 in Dundas, Vinton County, Ohio. She died on 24 Apr 1948 in McArthur, Ohio. She married Earl C. Bay, son of F. H. Bay and Ida Trimmer on 20 Dec 1906 in Vinton County, Ohio. He was born in 1880 in Hamden. He died before 24 Apr 1948.

9.    **SARAH MARGARET**[3] **TIMMS** (Richard[2], John B.[1]) was born on 15 May 1844 in Wirt County, Virginia. She died on 23 Dec 1921 in Mahaska County, Iowa. She married Joseph Harvey Evans, son of Jacob Evans and Mary (unknown) on 25 Nov 1886 in Mahaska County, Iowa. He was born on 10 Aug 1822 in Maryland. He died on 09 Jul 1908 in Oskaloosa, Mahaska County, Iowa.

More About Sarah Margaret Timms:
Burial: Coal Creek Cemetery, Mahaska, Iowa

More About Joseph Harvey Evans:
Burial: Coal Creek Cemetery, Mahaska, Iowa

Joseph Harvey Evans and Sarah Margaret Timms had the following child:
25.    i.    JOSEPHINE HELEN[4] EVANS was born on 09 Aug 1888 in Mahaska County, Iowa. She died in Jul 1977 in Missoula, Montana. She married Roy Roscoe Herbig on 09 Nov 1910 in Mahaska County, Iowa. He was born on 23 Feb 1891 in Mahaska County, Iowa. He died in Feb 1974 in San Diego, California.

10.    **FRANCES B.**[3] **TIMMS** (Richard[2], John B.[1]) was born on 08 Jun 1848 in Virginia. She died in 1920 in Long Beach, California. She married William S. England on 24 Mar 1869 in Vinton County, Ohio.

William S. England and Frances B. Timms had the following children:
    MAY[4] ENGLAND was born on 20 Aug 1869 in Vinton County, Ohio.

    WILLIAM ENGLAND was born on 07 Mar 1874 in Vinton County, Ohio.

**Generation 4**

11.    **EMMA L.**[4] **MOREHEAD** (Harriet L.[3] Timms, Richard[2] Timms, John B.[1] Timms) was born on 09 Sep 1859 in Virginia. She died on 12 Apr 1922 in West Virginia. She married George W. Stephens on 19 May 1881 in Wirt County, West Virginia. He was born on 06 Jul 1852 in Virginia. He died on 21 Sep 1916 in West Virginia.

More About Emma L. Morehead:
Burial: Limestone Cemetery, Wood County, West Virginia

More About George W. Stephens:
Burial: Limestone Cemetery, Wood County, West Virginia

George W. Stephens and Emma L. Morehead had the following children:

i.   CHARLES E.[5] STEPHENS was born on 31 Mar 1882 in West Virginia. He died on 25 Mar 1904 in West Virginia.

26.   ii. DELLA A. STEPHENS was born in 1886 in Wood County, West Virginia. She died in 1915 in Wood County, West Virginia. She married Charles M. Brown on 17 Aug 1910 in Wood County, West Virginia. He was born in 1881 in Wood County, West Virginia. He died in 1962 in Wood County, West Virginia.

iii.   RONNA B. STEPHENS was born on 17 Dec 1894 in West Virginia. She died in May 1975 in Wood County, West Virginia.

iv.   ALBERT C. STEPHENS was born on 11 Nov 1897 in Wood County, West Virginia. He died on 19 Mar 1898 in Wood County, West Virginia.

12.   **CHARLES ANDREW**[4] **MOREHEAD** (Harriet L.[3] Timms, Richard[2] Timms, John B.[1] Timms) was born in Oct 1860 in Wirt County, Virginia. He married (1) **JOSEPHINE DEEM** on 08 Oct 1885 in Wood County, West Virginia. She was born in Apr 1867 in Wood County, West Virginia. He married (2) **LULU MAY ROBERTS** on 12 Feb 1919 in Wood County, West Virginia. She was born about 1867 in Wirt County, West Virginia. She died in 1928.

Charles Andrew Morehead and Josephine Deem had the following children:

i.   LENA[5] MOREHEAD was born in Apr 1887 in West Virginia.

ii.   EVERETT MOREHEAD was born in Jul 1889 in West Virginia.

iii.   PERRY MOREHEAD.

13.   **RHODA ISABELLA**[4] **BARNETT** (Mary Jane[3] Timms, Richard[2] Timms, John B.[1] Timms) was born on 13 Feb 1866 in Dundas, Ohio. She died on 04 Nov 1957 in Mahaska County, Iowa. She married Calvin W. Woodruff on 23 Oct 1889 in Vinton County, Ohio. He was born on 02 Apr 1837 in Muskingum County, ohio. He died in 1916.

More About Rhoda Isabella Barnett:
Burial: Forest Cemetery, Mahaska County, Iowa

More About Calvin W. Woodruff:
Burial: Forest Cemetery, Mahaska County, Iowa

Calvin W. Woodruff and Rhoda Isabella Barnett had the following child:
27.   i. ROSCOE BARNETT[5] WOODRUFF was born on 09 Feb 1891 in Mahaska County, Iowa. He died on 24 Jul 1975 in San Antonio, Texas. He married Alice Wallace Gray on 21 May 1917. She was born on 21 Mar 1890 in Texas. She died in Dec 1985 in San Antonio, Texas.

14.   **BENJAMIN FRANKLIN**[4] **BARNETT** (Mary Jane[3] Timms, Richard[2] Timms, John B.[1] Timms) was born on 30 Apr 1868 in Vinton County, Ohio. He died on 10 Jun 1949 in Stockton, California. He married Malinda Louella Adair on 23 Nov 1904 in Mahaska County, Iowa. She was born on 26 Mar 1887 in Mahaska County, Iowa. She died on 04 Jan 1954 in Stockton, California.

More About Benjamin Franklin Barnett:
Burial: Park View Mausoleum, Stockton, California

More About Malinda Louella Adair:

Burial: Park View Mausoleum, Stockton, California

Benjamin Franklin Barnett and Malinda Louella Adair had the following children:

28.     i.   ZELLA MAXINE[5] BARNETT was born on 18 Jan 1906 in Mahaska County, Iowa. She died on 08 Nov 1993 in San Joaquin County, California. She married BYRON WELLINGTON CLAYWORTH. He was born on 22 Jul 1902 in Mahaska County, Iowa. He died on 12 May 1950 in San Joaquin County, California.

     ii.   EVELYN BEATRICE BARNETT was born on 13 Jul 1907 in Mahaska County, Iowa. She died on 24 May 1997 in Parkersburg, West Virginia. She married Alfred Lupkie Ammerman on 22 Jul 1926 in Chickasaw County, Iowa. He was born on 06 Apr 1904 in Franklin County, Iowa. He died on 13 Dec 1972 in Franklin County, Iowa.

        More About Evelyn Beatrice Barnett:
        Burial: Hampton Cemetery, Franklin County, Iowa

     iii.   MARY CAMILLE BARNETT was born on 28 Sep 1908 in Mahaska County, Iowa. She married Edwin Everett Carver on 11 Oct 1930 in Reno, Nevada. He was born on 19 Jan 1902. He died on 12 Aug 1957 in California.

        More About Mary Camille Barnett:
        Burial: Park View Cemetery, Stockton, California

15.    **ANNA LAURIE[4] BARNETT** (Mary Jane[3] Timms, Richard[2] Timms, John B.[1] Timms) was born on 14 Jul 1873 in Vinton County, Ohio. She died on 04 Aug 1959 in Vinton County, Ohio. She married George E. Pugh on 02 Aug 1891 in Vinton County, Ohio. He was born on 13 Oct 1861 in Gallipolis Ferry, West Virginia. He died on 10 Sep 1959 in Vinton County, Ohio.

More About Anna Laurie Barnett:
Burial: Elk Cemetery, Dundas, Ohio

More About George E. Pugh:
Burial: Elk Cemetery, Dundas, Ohio

George E. Pugh and Anna Laurie Barnett had the following children:

     i.   EDNA MORLEY[5] PUGH was born on 31 Dec 1891 in Summit County, Ohio. She died on 19 Sep 1984.

     ii.   HARRIE HAYS PUGH was born on 17 May 1895 in Vinton County, Ohio. She died in Sep 1988 in Washington County, Ohio. She married Clarence B. Shartz on 23 Oct 1919. He was born in 1892. He died on 22 May 1950 in Washington County, Ohio.

16.    **MINNIE VICTORIA[4] TIMMS** (John Bibbee[3], Richard[2], John B.[1]) was born on 21 Jan 1871 in Wirt County, West Virginia. She died on 11 Sep 1961 in Worthington, Ohio. She married Edward Warren Salts, son of George Salts and Mary Jane McKibbon on 18 Oct 1892 in Vinton County, Ohio. He was born on 05 Jul 1868 in Clinton Township, Vinton County, Ohio. He died on 02 Jan 1943 in Orange Township, Delaware County, Ohio.

More About Minnie Victoria Timms:
Burial: Elk Cemetery, Dundas, Ohio

More About Edward Warren Salts:

Burial: 05 Jan 1943 in Elk Cemetery, Dundas, Ohio
Cause Of Death:  Cerebral Hemorrhage
Living In: 1900 in Allegheny County, Pennsylvania
Occupation: Machinist

Edward Warren Salts and Minnie Victoria Timms had the following children:
   i. RALPH EDWIN[5] SALTS was born on 28 Jun 1893 in Pittsburgh, Pennsylvania. He died on 23
    Sep 1955 in Corapolis, Pennsylvania. He married Mary Agnes Garvey on 23 May 1918 in
    Pittsburgh, Pennsylvania. She was born on 14 Feb 1893 in Beaver Falls, Pennsylvania.
    She died on 21 Oct 1982 in Corapolis, Pennsylvania.

    MARY ELIZABETH SALTS was born on 18 Aug 1894 in Pittsburgh, Pennsylvania. She
    died on 07 Jun 1979. She married Edward A. Wright, son of William E. Wright and Anna
    Bell Davault on 20 Nov 1918 in Franklin County, ohio. He was born in Worthington, Ohio.

    RAYMOND WALLACE SALTS was born on 05 Jul 1897 in Allegheny County,
    Pennsylvania. He died in Allegheny County, Pennsylvania.

    EDWARD WARREN SALTS was born on 20 Jan 1907 in Worthington, Ohio. He died on 09
    Apr 1999 in Columbus, Ohio. He married Ethel May Evans on 27 Jun 1934 in Delaware
    County, Ohio. She was born on 19 Sep 1909 in Delaware County, Ohio.

17. **JOHN FRANKLIN**[4] **TIMMS** (John Bibbee[3], Richard[2], John B.[1]) was born on 11 Oct 1879 in Vinton County,
  Ohio. He died on 04 Apr 1945 in Vinton County, Ohio. He married **ELIZABETH AUSTIN**. She was born
  about 1883 in Vinton County, Ohio. She died on 06 Jun 1955 in Vinton County, Ohio.


More About John Franklin Timms:
Burial: Elk Cemetery, Dundas, Ohio
Cause Of Death: Fractured Skull
Occupation:  Farmer

More About Elizabeth Austin: Burial:

Elk Cemetery, Dundas, Ohio

John Franklin Timms and Elizabeth Austin had the following children:
   i. REFFORD[5] TIMMS was born on 25 Nov 1907 in Jackson County, Ohio. He died on 28 Mar
    1937 in Columbus, Ohio.

    More About Refford Timms: Cause
    Of Death: Skull Fracture

   ii. EARL A. TIMMS was born on 24 Oct 1904 in Vinton County, Ohio. He died on 21 Oct 1989
    in Butler County, Ohio. He married DORA GEORGE. She was born on 14 Jul 1903 in
    Creola, Vinton County, Ohio. She died on 14 May 1992 in Butler County, Ohio.

   iii. ANNIE LUCILLE TIMMS was born on 08 Sep 1913 in Vinton County, Ohio. She married
    Thomas J. Rannells on 27 May 1939 in Vinton County, Ohio. He was born on 29 Jan 1906
    in Vinton County, Ohio. He died on 20 Jan 2003 in Vinton County, Ohio.

   iv. MAXINE TIMMS was born on 03 Jun 1916 in Vinton County, Ohio. She died on 13 Jun
    2003 in Florida. She married Verner D. Honchell on 09 Oct 1937 in Vinton

County, Ohio. He was born on 15 Feb 1915 in Ohio.

    v.   ALICE GRACE TIMMS was born on 22 Sep 1918 in Vinton County, Ohio. She married KENNETH WITHROW.

18.   **AMY LOUISE**[4] **TIMMS** (Ezra Quimby[3], Richard[2], John B.[1]) was born on 24 Mar 1868 in Clinton Township, Vinton County, Ohio. She died on 04 May 1959 in Vinton County, Ohio. She married Willis Garvin Salts, son of John Salts and Ivy Hoffiner on 21 Jun 1888 in Vinton County, Ohio. He was born on 02 Mar 1863 in Vinton County, Ohio. He died on 10 Nov 1910 in Vinton County, Ohio.

More About Amy Louise Timms:
Burial: Hixon Cemetery, Vinton County, Ohio

More About Willis Garvin Salts:
Burial: 12 Nov 1910 in Hixon Cemetery, Vinton County, Ohio
Occupation: Farmer

Willis Garvin Salts and Amy Louise Timms had the following children:
    i.   SYLVIA MAE[5] SALTS was born on 02 Sep 1889 in Vinton County, Ohio. She died on 3 Oct 1896 in Vinton County, Ohio.

31.   ii. LULA CECIL SALTS was born on 16 Jan 1891 in Dundas, Vinton County, Ohio. She died on 14 Oct 1944 in Marion, Ohio. She married (1) ELISHA BARTON HAMMON, son of John C. Hammon and Emma Taylor on 24 Dec 1915 in Franklin County, ohio. He was born on 28 Feb 1876 in Gallia County, Ohio. He died on 31 Oct 1921 in Marion County, Ohio. She married (2) JOHN SMITH, son of Levi Smith and Margaret Nicholson on 20 Oct 1923 in Marion County, Ohio. He was born in 1881 in Appalache, North Carolina.

32.   iii. INA FAY SALTS was born on 18 Jul 1893 in Vinton County, Ohio. She died on 09 Aug 1987 in Columbus, Ohio. She married James Emmett Wortman on 30 Oct 1919. He was born on 30 Oct 1891 in Vinton County, Ohio. He died on 24 Apr 1979 in Jackson County, Ohio.

    iv.   ROY TIMMS SALTS was born on 25 Jun 1895 in Vinton County, Ohio. He died in Nov 1895 in Macomb County, Michigan.

32.   v. OTTO GUY SALTS was born on 03 Apr 1897 in Dundas, Vinton County, Ohio. He died on 16 Dec 1955. He married Mildred Alberta Roof on 29 Apr 1928 in Vinton County, Ohio. She was born on 25 Mar 1910. She died on 02 Jan 1964.

33.   vi. KENNETH DUMONT SALTS was born on 11 Feb 1899 in Vinton County, Ohio. He died on 01 Jan 1987 in Vinton County, Ohio. He married HELEN RUTH MASON. She was born on 20 May 1914. She died in Feb 1966.

    vii.   ROBERT FENTON SALTS was born on 21 Nov 1900 in Vinton County, Ohio. He died on 12 Aug 1980. He married Edith Murray on 19 Apr 1924. She was born on 31 Oct 1905. She died in Apr 1985 in Franklin County, ohio.

    viii.   EARL RAYMOND SALTS was born on 12 Dec 1904 in Vinton County, Ohio. He died in Dec 1970 in Jackson County, Ohio. He married NELLIE CANTER. She was born on 5 Jun 1902. She died in Jan 1987 in Jackson County, Ohio.

    ix.   SYBIL IONA SALTS was born on 05 Dec 1906 in Vinton County, Ohio. She married

Boyd Bobo on 19 Apr 1924. He was born on 05 Aug 1904. He died in Jun 1979 in Vinton County, Ohio.

    x.    EZRA GARVIN SALTS was born on 13 Dec 1910 in Vinton County, Ohio. He died on 27 Jun 1988 in Vinton County, Ohio. He married Verla May Potts on 02 Apr 1932.

More About Ezra Garvin Salts:
Burial: Hixon Cemetery, Vinton County, Ohio

19.    **HENRY MILTON**[4] **TIMMS** (Ezra Quimby[3], Richard[2], John B.[1]) was born on 31 Mar 1870 in Dundas, Vinton County, Ohio. He died on 15 Feb 1953 in Wellston, Ohio. He married Anna Gunning, daughter of Orville Gunning and Catherine (unknown) on 29 Mar 1889. She was born on 23 Oct 1864 in Vinton County, Ohio. She died on 17 Jun 1943 in Clinton, Vinton County, Ohio.

More About Henry Milton Timms:
Burial: 18 Feb 1953 in Elk Cemetery, McArthur, Ohio
Cause Of Death: ; Gangrene of left leg
Occupation: Farmer

More About Anna Gunning:
Burial: 20 Jun 1943 in Elk Cemetery, McArthur, Ohio

Henry Milton Timms and Anna Gunning had the following child:
    i.    HELEN C.[5] TIMMS was born on 25 Sep 1902 in Vinton County, Ohio. She married Miller (unknown) in Sep 1946.

20.    **JAMES W.**[4] **TIMMS** (Ezra Quimby[3], Richard[2], John B.[1]) was born on 09 Mar 1872 in Clinton Township, Vinton County, Ohio. He died on 02 Mar 1961. He married Sarah J. Bobo, daughter of Thomas W. Bobo and Mary E. (unknown) on 30 Jan 1895 in Vinton County, Ohio. She was born about 1865 in Ohio.

More About James W. Timms:
Occupation: ; Farmer

James W. Timms and Sarah J. Bobo had the following child:
    i.    ALTA M.[5] TIMMS was born on 11 Jan 1896. She married (UNKNOWN) PERRINER.

21.    **ANNA LUELLA**[4] **TIMMS** (Ezra Quimby[3], Richard[2], John B.[1]) was born on 23 Dec 1873 in Clinton Township, Vinton County, Ohio. She died on 02 Jan 1949 in Clinton Township, Vinton County, Ohio. She married Samuel Russell on 01 Jan 1896 in Vinton County, Ohio. He died after 02 Jan 1949.

More About Anna Luella Timms:
Burial: 05 Jan 1949 in Elk Cemetery, McArthur, Ohio
Cause Of Death: Cerebral Hemorrhage

Samuel Russell and Anna Luella Timms had the following child:
    i.    NELLIE E.[5] RUSSELL was born on 04 Nov 1896. She married ROY DYE.

22.    **CHARLES VANCE**[4] **TIMMS** (Ezra Quimby[3], Richard[2], John B.[1]) was born on 19 Dec 1875 in Vinton County, Ohio. He died on 01 Mar 1961 in Hocking County, Ohio. He married Maggie Elizabeth

Martin, daughter of Albert Martin and Mary Alice (unknown) on 01 Jan 1918 in Vinton County, Ohio. She was born on 03 Jan 1889 in Vinton County, Ohio. She died on 17 Jan 1939 in Clinton, Vinton County, Ohio.


More About Charles Vance Timms:
Burial: Hixon Cemetery, Vinton County, Ohio
Occupation:  Farmer, Vinton County, Ohio

More About Maggie Elizabeth Martin:
Burial: 19 Jan 1939 in Hixon Cemetery, Vinton County, Ohio
Cause Of Death: Bowel Obstruction

Charles Vance Timms and Maggie Elizabeth Martin had the following children:
34.     i.     JOHN MARTIN[5] TIMMS was born on 27 Feb 1919 in Vinton County, Ohio. He died on 10 Aug 1946 in Vinton County, Ohio. He married LILLIE LOUISE PIERCE. She was born on 07 Jul 1923 in Ohio. She died on 23 May 2006 in Vinton County, Ohio.

    iii.     ALICE MINERVA TIMMS was born on 18 Apr 1921 in Vinton County, Ohio. She died on 25 Oct 1953 in Dundas, Ohio.


More About Alice Minerva Timms:
Burial: 27 Oct 1953 in Hixon Cemetery, Dundas, Ohio


23.     **GEORGE BARNETT[4] TIMMS** (Ezra Quimby[3], Richard[2], John B.[1]) was born on 29 Jul 1878 in Dundas, Clinton Township, Vinton County, Ohio. He died on 10 Sep 1916. He married (1) **IRMA PIERCE** on 06 Sep 1902. He married (2) **SADIE WORTMAN** on 17 Sep 1907 in Hamilton, Ohio. He married (3) **SARAH ELIZABETH MONROE**, daughter of Charles B. Monroe and Eliza Westcott on 17 Sep 1907 in Cincinnati, Ohio. She was born on 13 Feb 1878 in Tuscola, Illinois. She died on 07 Jul 1940.


More About George Barnett Timms:
Occupation: Railroad, Freeport, Illinois

George Barnett Timms and Irma Pierce had the following children:
    i. BARNETT P.[5] TIMMS was born on 01 Sep 1902. He died in Aug 1969 in Jefferson county, Ohio.

    ii.     ELIZABETH B. TIMMS.


Notes for Sadie Wortman:
Ohio Marriage Records gives name as Sadie Enlow.

George Barnett Timms and Sarah Elizabeth Monroe had the following child:
    iii. BLANCHE E. TIMMS was born on 02 Sep 1910. She died in Aug 1991. She married Hurlbut Leslie Baumgardner, son of Hurlbut L. Baumgardner and Alice Belding Young on 03 Sep 1937. He was born in Aug 1919. He died on 26 Sep 1981 in Oakland, Michigan.

24.     **SUSAN GENEVA[4] TIMMS** (Ezra Quimby[3], Richard[2], John B.[1]) was born on 04 Feb 1886 in Dundas, Vinton County, Ohio. She died on 24 Apr 1948 in McArthur, Ohio. She married Earl C. Bay, son of F. H. Bay and Ida Trimmer on 20 Dec 1906 in Vinton County, Ohio. He was born in 1880 in Hamden. He died before 24 Apr 1948.

More About Susan Geneva Timms:
Burial: 27 Apr 1948 in McArthur, Ohio
Cause Of Death: Cerebral Hemorrhage

More About Earl C. Bay:
Occupation: Farmer

Earl C. Bay and Susan Geneva Timms had the following children:
  i.    VIRGINIA[5] BAY was born on 02 Oct 1907.

  ii.   ROBERT MILTON BAY was born on 09 Dec 1910.

  iii.  JUDY BAY.

25.   **JOSEPHINE HELEN[4] EVANS** (Sarah Margaret[3] Timms, Richard[2] Timms, John B.[1] Timms) was born on 09 Aug 1888 in Mahaska County, Iowa. She died in Jul 1977 in Missoula, Montana. She married Roy Roscoe Herbig on 09 Nov 1910 in Mahaska County, Iowa. He was born on 23 Feb 1891 in Mahaska County, Iowa. He died in Feb 1974 in San Diego, California.

Roy Roscoe Herbig and Josephine Helen Evans had the following children:
  i.    HELEN LOUISE[5] HERBIG was born on 03 Oct 1911 in Cavalier County, North dakota. She married BENJAMIN F. CLARKE.

  ii.   ANNA ALICE HERBIG was born on 10 May 1913. She married (UNKNOWN) WALKER.

  iii.  PHILLIP HOBART HERBIG was born on 12 Oct 1918 in Mahaska County, Iowa.

  iv.   CARL EVANS HERBIG was born on 23 Jul 1919. He died in 1995.

  v.    MARY JOSEPHINE HERBIG was born on 30 Dec 1920. She married (UNKNOWN) HILL.

  vi.   ROY ROSCOE HERBIG was born on 12 Aug 1922 in Mahaska County, Iowa. He died in 1955.

  vii.  HAROLD HUBERT HERBIG was born on 20 Nov 1924 in Mahaska County, Iowa.

  viii. DON JOSEPH HERBIG was born on 27 Jan 1927 in Macomb County, Michigan.

**Generation 5**

26.   **DELLA A.[5] STEPHENS** (Emma L.[4] Morehead, Harriet L.[3] Timms, Richard[2] Timms, John B.[1] Timms) was born in 1886 in Wood County, West Virginia. She died in 1915 in Wood County, West Virginia. She married Charles M. Brown on 17 Aug 1910 in Wood County, West Virginia. He was born in 1881 in Wood County, West Virginia. He died in 1962 in Wood County, West Virginia.

More About Della A. Stephens:
Burial: Limestone Cemetery, Wood County, West Virginia

More About Charles M. Brown:
Burial: Limestone Cemetery, Wood County, West Virginia

Charles M. Brown and Della A. Stephens had the following children:
  i.    MELVIN[6] BROWN was born about 1912 in West Virginia.

    ii.    FORREST CLAYTON BROWN was born on 17 Jun 1915 in Wood County, West Virginia.

27.    **ROSCOE BARNETT**[5] **WOODRUFF** (Rhoda Isabella[4] Barnett, Mary Jane[3] Timms, Richard[2] Timms, John B.[1] Timms) was born on 09 Feb 1891 in Mahaska County, Iowa. He died on 24 Jul 1975 in San Antonio, Texas. He married Alice Wallace Gray on 21 May 1917. She was born on 21 Mar 1890 in Texas. She died in Dec 1985 in San Antonio, Texas.

More About Roscoe Barnett Woodruff:
Burial: Fort Sam Houston Cemetery, San Antonio, Texas

More About Alice Wallace Gray:
Burial: Fort Sam Houston Cemetery, San Antonio, Texas

Roscoe Barnett Woodruff and Alice Wallace Gray had the following children:
    i.    ROSCOE BARNETT[6] WOODRUFF.

    ii.    DOROTHY GRAY WOODRUFF. She married Robert John Daniels on 22 Apr 1946 in San Antonio, Texas.

28.    **ZELLA MAXINE**[5] **BARNETT** (Benjamin Franklin[4], Mary Jane[3] Timms, Richard[2] Timms, John B.[1] Timms) was born on 18 Jan 1906 in Mahaska County, Iowa. She died on 08 Nov 1993 in San Joaquin County, California. She married **BYRON WELLINGTON CLAYWORTH**. He was born on 22 Jul 1902 in Mahaska County, Iowa. He died on 12 May 1950 in San Joaquin County, California.

More About Zella Maxine Barnett:
Burial: Park View Cemetery, Stockton, California

More About Byron Wellington Clayworth:
Burial: Park View Cemetery, Stockton, California

Byron Wellington Clayworth and Zella Maxine Barnett had the following children:
    i.    ROSAMUND FRANCINE[6] CLAYWORTH was born on 02 May 1927 in Stockton, California. She died in 1995 in Ensenada, Mexico. She married ROBERT JEROME. He was born on 29 Jun 1913. He died in Sep 1981 in San Bernadeno County, California.

    ii.    JOHN WELLINGTON CLAYWORTH was born on 24 Aug 1928 in Stockton, California. He died on 14 Apr 1989 in Sacramento, California.

29.    **RALPH EDWIN**[5] **SALTS** (Minnie Victoria[4] Timms, John Bibbee[3] Timms, Richard[2] Timms, John B.[1] Timms) was born on 28 Jun 1893 in Pittsburgh, Pennsylvania. He died on 23 Sep 1955 in Corapolis, Pennsylvania. He married Mary Agnes Garvey on 23 May 1918 in Pittsburgh, Pennsylvania. She was born on 14 Feb 1893 in Beaver Falls, Pennsylvania. She died on 21 Oct 1982 in Corapolis, Pennsylvania.

Ralph Edwin Salts and Mary Agnes Garvey had the following children:
36.    i.    JAMES GARVEY[6] SALTS was born on 11 Jan 1920 in Pittsburgh, Pennsylvania. He died on 25 Jul 1998 in Minneapolis, Minnesota. He married Shirley Jean Glanville on 30 Oct 1944 in Douglas County, Wisconsin. She was born on 16 Jul 1927 in Madison, Wisconsin.

    ii.    KATHERINE ELIZABETH SALTS was born on 06 Aug 1922 in Sewickley, Pennsylvania.

She married (1) D ORN WELLINGTON DODD on 22 Jan 1944 in Corapolis, Pennsylvania. He was born on 02 May 1921 in Ellwood City, Pennsylvania. She married (2) ROBERT BRYANT DANZEY on 07 Jul 1951 in Pittsburgh, Pennsylvania. He was born on 13 Oct 1921 in Indianola, Pennsylvania. He died on 18 Aug 1992 in Phoenix, Arizona.

    iii.    MARGARET EDITH SALTS was born on 02 Nov 1923 in Sewickley, Pennsylvania. She married Robert George Wynn on 01 Oct 1948 in Pittsburgh, Pennsylvania. He was born on 29 May 1918 in Glenwillard, Pennsylvavia.

30.    **LULA CECIL[5] SALTS** (Amy Louise[4] Timms, Ezra Quimby[3] Timms, Richard[2] Timms, John B.[1] Timms) was born on 16 Jan 1891 in Dundas, Vinton County, Ohio. She died on 14 Oct 1944 in Marion, Ohio. She married (1) **ELISHA BARTON HAMMON**, son of John C. Hammon and Emma Taylor on 24 Dec 1915 in Franklin County, ohio. He was born on 28 Feb 1876 in Gallia County, Ohio. He died on 31 Oct 1921 in Marion County, Ohio. She married (2) **JOHN SMITH**, son of Levi Smith and Margaret Nicholson on 20 Oct 1923 in Marion County, Ohio. He was born in 1881 in Appalache, North Carolina.

More About Lula Cecil Salts:
Burial: 17 Oct 1944 in Marion Cemetery, Marion, Ohio
Cause Of Death: Cerebral Hemorrhage

Elisha Barton Hammon and Lula Cecil Salts had the following children:
    i.    MARY[6] HAMMON.

    ii.    RALPH B. HAMMON was born on 06 Aug 1916 in Marion County, Ohio. He died on 06 Oct 1988 in Marion County, Ohio. He married Delores L. Whaley on 02 Feb 1940. She was born on 23 Apr 1918 in Marion County, Ohio. She died in Aug 1993 in Marion County, Ohio.

31.    **INA FAY[5] SALTS** (Amy Louise[4] Timms, Ezra Quimby[3] Timms, Richard[2] Timms, John B.[1] Timms) was born on 18 Jul 1893 in Vinton County, Ohio. She died on 09 Aug 1987 in Columbus, Ohio. She married James Emmett Wortman on 30 Oct 1919. He was born on 30 Oct 1891 in Vinton County, Ohio. He died on 24 Apr 1979 in Jackson County, Ohio.

More About Ina Fay Salts:
Burial: Hixon Cemetery, Vinton County, Ohio

More About James Emmett Wortman: Burial:
Hixon Cemetery, Vinton County, Ohio

James Emmett Wortman and Ina Fay Salts had the following children:
    i.    ARMINDA LOUISE[6] WORTMAN was born on 16 Aug 1920 in Vinton County, Ohio. She married Sturgill Asbury Summers on 21 Oct 1939 in Boyd County, Kentucky. He was born on 08 Aug 1915 in Roane County, West Virginia. He died on 25 Oct 1993 in Clark County, Ohio.

    ii.    THELMA MARIE WORTMAN was born on 31 Jan 1924 in Vinton County, Ohio. She married Beryl McMasters on 28 Oct 1950 in Clark County, Ohio. He was born on 18 Oct 1927.

32.    **OTTO GUY[5] SALTS** (Amy Louise[4] Timms, Ezra Quimby[3] Timms, Richard[2] Timms, John B.[1] Timms) was born on 03 Apr 1897 in Dundas, Vinton County, Ohio. He died on 16 Dec 1955. He married

Mildred Alberta Roof on 29 Apr 1928 in Vinton County, Ohio. She was born on 25 Mar 1910. She died on 02 Jan 1964.


More About Otto Guy Salts:
Burial: Hixon Cemetery, Vinton County, Ohio

More About Mildred Alberta Roof:
Burial: Hixon Cemetery, Vinton County, Ohio

Otto Guy Salts and Mildred Alberta Roof had the following children:
  i. CARL EUGENE[6] SALTS was born on 14 Jul 1929. He died on 06 Oct 1998.


    More About Carl Eugene Salts: Burial:
    Hixon Cemetery, Dundas, Ohio


  ii. RALPH EDMOND SALTS was born on 01 Jun 1933. He died in 1934.


    More About Ralph Edmond Salts: Burial:
    Hixon Cemetery, Dundas, Ohio


  iii. BARBARA SUE SALTS was born on 19 Apr 1938. She died in 1943.

  iv. CONNIE LEE SALTS was born on 03 Jun 1951. She died in 1984.


33. **KENNETH DUMONT[5] SALTS** (Amy Louise[4] Timms, Ezra Quimby[3] Timms, Richard[2] Timms, John B.[1] Timms) was born on 11 Feb 1899 in Vinton County, Ohio. He died on 01 Jan 1987 in Vinton County, Ohio. He married **HELEN RUTH MASON**. She was born on 20 May 1914. She died in Feb 1966.


More About Kenneth Dumont Salts:
Burial: Elk Cemetery, Dundas, Ohio

Kenneth Dumont Salts and Helen Ruth Mason had the following child:
  i. CLARENCE ALLEN[6] SALTS was born on 29 Apr 1941 in Vinton County, Ohio. He died on 29 Apr 1941 in Vinton County, Ohio.


34. **JOHN MARTIN[5] TIMMS** (Charles Vance[4], Ezra Quimby[3], Richard[2], John B.[1]) was born on 27 Feb 1919 in Vinton County, Ohio. He died on 10 Aug 1946 in Vinton County, Ohio. He married **LILLIE LOUISE PIERCE**. She was born on 07 Jul 1923 in Ohio. She died on 23 May 2006 in Vinton County, Ohio.


Notes for John Martin Timms:
Killed in an accidental explosion at Austin Powder Company in Vinton County, Ohio.

John Martin Timms and Lillie Louise Pierce had the following child:
37. i. FRANKLIN EUGENE[6] TIMMS was born on 03 May 1940 in Dundas, Ohio. He married EVLYN MARIE STEWART. She was born on 17 Dec 1944 in South Perry, Ohio.


35. **BLANCHE E.[5] TIMMS** (George Barnett[4], Ezra Quimby[3], Richard[2], John B.[1]) was born on 02 Sep 1910. She died in Aug 1991. She married Hurlbut Leslie Baumgardner, son of Hurlbut L.

Baumgardner and Alice Belding Young on 03 Sep 1937. He was born in Aug 1919. He died on 26 Sep 1981 in Oakland, Michigan.

Hurlbut Leslie Baumgardner and Blanche E. Timms had the following child:
  i.   HURLBUT LESLIE[6] BAUMGARDNER was born in Aug 1945. He died on 28 Jan 1996. He married (UNKNOWN) SPRING. He married (UNKNOWN) TOLBERT.

---

**Generation 6**

36.  **JAMES GARVEY[6] SALTS** (Ralph Edwin[5], Minnie Victoria[4] Timms, John Bibbee[3] Timms, Richard[2] Timms, John B.[1] Timms) was born on 11 Jan 1920 in Pittsburgh, Pennsylvania. He died on 25 Jul 1998 in Minneapolis, Minnesota. He married Shirley Jean Glanville on 30 Oct 1944 in Douglas County, Wisconsin. She was born on 16 Jul 1927 in Madison, Wisconsin.

James Garvey Salts and Shirley Jean Glanville had the following child:
  i.   GARVEY JAMES[7] SALTS was born on 03 Jan 1947 in Sewickley, Pennsylvania. He died on 13 Feb 1947 in Sewickley, Pennsylvania.

37.  **FRANKLIN EUGENE[6] TIMMS** (John Martin[5], Charles Vance[4], Ezra Quimby[3], Richard[2], John B.[1]) was born on 03 May 1940 in Dundas, Ohio. He married **EVLYN MARIE STEWART**. She was born on 17 Dec 1944 in South Perry, Ohio.

Franklin Eugene Timms and Evlyn Marie Stewart had the following children:
38.  i.   ROBERT[7] TIMMS.  He married RENEE WOMELDORF.

39.  ii. JOHN MARTIN TIMMS was born on 04 Jan 1965 in Lancaster, Ohio. He married TOBBI ELLEN TAYLOR. She was born on 11 Jan 1963 in Sacramento, California.

---

**Generation 7**

38.  **ROBERT[7] TIMMS** (Franklin Eugene[6], John Martin[5], Charles Vance[4], Ezra Quimby[3], Richard[2], John B.[1]). He married **RENEE WOMELDORF**.
Robert Timms and Renee Womeldorf had the following children:
  i.   DANIELLE[8] TIMMS.

  ii.   CASSANDRA TIMMS.

  iii.   ROBERT RYAN TIMMS.

39.  **JOHN MARTIN[7] TIMMS** (Franklin Eugene[6], John Martin[5], Charles Vance[4], Ezra Quimby[3], Richard[2], John B.[1]) was born on 04 Jan 1965 in Lancaster, Ohio. He married **TOBBI ELLEN TAYLOR**. She was born on 11 Jan 1963 in Sacramento, California.

John Martin Timms and Tobbi Ellen Taylor had the following children:
  i.   IAN CONNER[8] TIMMS was born on 20 Mar 1992 in Chillicothe, Ohio.

  ii.   MARY KATHERINE TAYLOR TIMMS was born on 30 Mar 1998 in Chillicothe, Ohio.

NOTES: